The Economic Efficiency of Financial Markets

The Economic Efficiency of Financial Markets

Jan Mossin

Lexington Books
D.C. Heath and Company
Lexington, Massachusetts
Toronto

Library of Congress Cataloging in Publication Data

Mossin, Jan.
 The economic efficiency of financial markets.

 1. Finance—Mathematical models. 2. Uncertainty—Mathematical models. 3. Welfare economics—Mathematical models. I. Title.
HG173.M644   332.6   76-28674
ISBN 0-669-01004-9

Published simultaneously in Canada

Printed in the United States of America

International Standard Book Number: 0-669-01004-9

Library of Congress Catalog Card Number:76-28674

Contents

List of Figures   vii

List of Tables   ix

Preface   xi

Part I   *Preliminaries*   1

Chapter 1   The Economic Setting   3

Chapter 2   The Concept of Efficiency   7

Part II   *Complete Markets*   15

Chapter 3   State Contingent Claims   21

Chapter 4   Complete Stock Markets   29

Part III   *Distributive Efficiency*   41

Chapter 5   Allocation of Securities versus Allocation of In-
                come   45

Chapter 6   Attainability   55

Chapter 7   Separation   65

Chapter 8   Market Optimality   73

Chapter 9   Capital Structure Theory   83

Part IV   *Efficiency of Investment*   95

Chapter 10   Share Price Maximization   99

Chapter 11   Diamond's Model   103

Chapter 12   Mean-Variance Valuation   111

Chapter 13   **Stiglitz's Model**   117

Chapter 14   **Stockholder Agreement**   127

Chapter 15   **Exclusive versus Competitive Investment**   133

Chapter 16   **Stockholder Disagreement**   143

                Index   157

                About the Author   159

List of Figures

1-1   Schematic Relationships among the
       Model Variables   4
2-1   Pareto-Optimality for Two Individuals   8
4-1   Probability Tree for Two Hypothetical
       Firms   39
6-1   Typical Representation of Sets of In-
       come Allocations in the Absence of
       Any Restrictions   57
6-2   Sets of Income Allocations Given That
       Conditions for Attainability Are Satis-
       fied   57
6-3   Sets of Income Allocations Given That
       Conditions for Market Optimality Are
       Satisfied   58
9-1   Opportunity Sets for an Individual in the
       Two-Firm Economy   85
9-2   Opportunity Sets in a Three-Dimension-
       al Income Space   90
12-1   Representation of Mean-Variance Effi-
       ciency   112
16-1   Market Demand Schedules for Two Poli-
       cy Choices   144

List of Tables

II-1	Example Situation: Three States of the World and Two Securities	18
3-1	Example: Investment Levels and Returns for Two Investment Plans	22
4-1	Numerical Example for Feasibility Relationships	31
4-2	Optimal Portfolios	31
4-3	Second-Period Output	33
4-4	Solution for Purchases of State Contingent Claims	33
4-5	Firms' Outputs as Functions of the State of the World	39
5-1	Income Vectors and Probability Distributions over Three States of the World	51
5-2	Pareto-Optimal Income Vectors	51
9-1	Two-Firm Economy	84
9-2	Two-Firm Economy with Identical Vectors of Second-Period Income	88
16-1	Numerical Example: Output Vectors for Two Investment Plans	148
16-2	Individuals' Probability Distributions for the Numerical Example	149
16-3	Resulting Allocations and Utilities for the Numerical Example	149
16-4	Implicit Prices for State Contingent Claims	155

Preface

The purpose of this little book is to bring together—in a coherent fashion—various contributions to the welfare theoretical aspects of modern capital market theory. That is, we shall examine the role of markets for financial claims in effecting, on the one hand, an efficient allocation of investment capital among investing-producing units, and, on the other hand, an efficient allocation of the resulting output (or return on investment) among consuming units.

The key feature that distinguishes the theory to be described here from traditional welfare theory is the presence of uncertainty—specifically, the uncertainty surrounding the outcome of production-investment decisions. Indeed, we could reformulate our subject matter as an examination of the question: Does the introduction of uncertainty affect the working of Adam Smith's "invisible hand" in promoting the general welfare and, if so, in what ways?

Although a more precise formulation of these problems remains to be given, it is clear that they are very basic and important ones. Unfortunately, they are also problems that, if they were to be approached in complete generality, would be virtually intractable. Consequently, certain abstractions and simplifications have to be made so as to give a workable mathematical model of the economy. These will be introduced and explained as we go along.

A quick thumbing through the pages that follow will reveal a fairly high content of mathematical paraphernalia. This is deliberate: one of the very objectives in writing the book has been to establish the derivation of the most important results in precise detail. Indeed, one of the reasons why the literature in the area often seems confusing and difficult to assimilate or reconcile is that important steps in the analysis have been omitted or treated with a handwave. In such cases, an attempt has been made to provide a reconstruction.

To avoid scaring away prospective readers there is a temptation to reduce the appearance of mathematical type by leaving out intermediate steps and replacing details of an argument by phrases such as "... it is easily shown that. ..." In the end, however, this is really doing the serious reader a disservice. The actual mathematical tools that are used should be familiar to most economists, however: liberal doses of calculus, including Lagrange multipliers; a smattering of linear algebra; the standard operations of probability. The presentation also presupposes familiarity with standard microeconomic theory including general equilibrium theory, as well as elements of the theory of choice and decision making under uncertainty.

It should be clear from the foregoing that the book is not intended as an introductory text. Rather, my ambition has been to provide a core text for more advanced graduate courses. As such, its coverage should find application in both finance and economics curricula.

The manuscript for the book has grown out of lecture notes from seminars in financial theory and markets at New York University's Graduate School of Business Administration and the Norwegian School of Economics and Business Administration, and I should like to acknowledge suggestions and corrections from a number of students in these seminars, as well as from students and faculty attending seminar and workshop presentations given at Columbia University, City University of New York, Princeton University, University of Toronto, Stockholm School of Economics, and Faculté Universitaire Catholique de Mons. More specifically, thanks are due to friends and colleagues with whom I have discussed topics incorporated in the book; these include K. Borch, K.P. Hagen, M.A. King, V.D. Norman, A. Sandmo, R.A. Schwartz, and D.K. Whitcomb.

Part I
Preliminaries

1

The Economic Setting

1.1. In this chapter we give a general characterization of the kind of economy with which we shall be concerned throughout and the kinds of allocation problems facing such an economy.

In making this characterization, it is important to keep in mind a clear distinction between the allocations that are *feasible* and the allocations that may be the result of some particular *allocative mechanism*, e.g., trading in a competitive market. In considering the former, and in evaluating the desirability of alternative allocations, we essentially adopt the view of a central planner, disregarding entirely the problem of actually implementing any given allocation. In considering the latter, we more adopt the attitude of the passive bystander, watching decisions being made and exchanges taking place.

1.2. The two most important simplifying features of our model are that there is a *single commodity* and that there are only *two periods* (referred to as the first and second period). The single commodity can be used either for first-period consumption or for investment in various productive activities, the output of which is to be used for second-period consumption.

A formulation of the model in terms of a single commodity means that all economic variables are measured in the same units and can be justified by an assumption of fixed technology (no substitution among inputs or outputs) and fixed relative prices among different goods. Under such an assumption, the "single good" should be thought of as an aggregate expressed in money terms, with, say, a dollar as unit of measurement. However, it may also be useful to think more literally in terms of a single physical good such as "corn," which can be used either for consumption today (as food) or for investment (as seed), the return on which is also the same physical good (as crop).

The two-period framework for the theory can probably only be justified by the simplification it affords. An extension to several periods is by no means trivial, as it would require the introduction of price uncertainty and a theory of the formation of expectations. By eliminating the need to consider such complicating features, however, it is possible to focus more sharply on some of the more basic functions of financial markets in the allocation process.

1.3. Figure 1-1 gives a schematic representation of the relationships

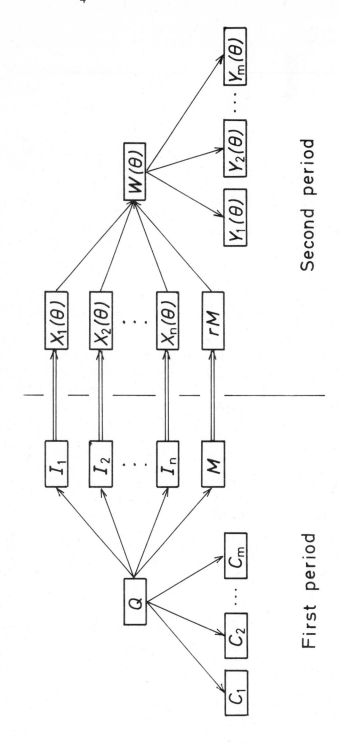

Figure 1-1. Schematic Relationships among the Model Variables.

among the variables of the model. The economy starts out with an initial total supply Q of the commodity; this supply is, from the point of view of a central planner, a given datum. There are m individuals (indexed $i = 1, \ldots, m$) whose first-period consumption is denoted C_i, and n "firms" or production functions (indexed $j = 1, \ldots, n$) whose level of input (or investment) is denoted I_j.

The second-period outputs of firms are denoted X_j; these are random variables whose probability distributions depend on the input levels I_j. In order to give a simple formulation of these relationships we shall assume that the uncertainty can be parametrized by means of a single random variable θ referred to as the "state of the world." That is, rather than working with a joint probability distribution for the X_js, we assume that they can all be written as functions of the same random variable θ. We then write the input-output relationship for firm j in the form of a "stochastic production function"

$$X_j(\theta) = \phi_j(I_j, \theta) \tag{1.1}$$

where $X_j(\theta)$ is output in state of the world θ given as a function of the firm's level of investment. It may be useful to think of (1.1) as representing a *family* of production functions, one for each state of the world. The functions ϕ_j are assumed to be strictly increasing, concave functions of I_j. We further assume that the random variable θ is discrete and has been suitably normalized to take on the integer values ($\theta = 1, \ldots, s$). The number of different states of the world, s, may be finite or infinite.

We also note that the formulation (1.1) excludes ordinary technological externalities in the sense of one firm's output being affected by other firms' input levels. *Stochastic dependence* among the X_js is, of course, not ruled out.

1.4. The n firms whose technology has been described so far will be referred to as the risky firms, despite the fact that we have not really excluded the possibility that some $X_j(\theta)$s might be the same for every θ. For explicitness, however, it is assumed that in addition to the risky firms there is available a riskless investment opportunity with a total level of investment denoted M. In general, it might seem most reasonable to write the second-period return as some (presumably concave) function of M; however, little of theoretical interest seems to come out of such a generalization and we shall therefore make the simplifying assumption of constant returns to scale so that second-period return is rM with r constant. For an individual, investment in the riskless opportunity is therefore just like putting money in a bank that pays an interest rate of $r - 1$. Thus, r represents one plus the risk free interest rate; this must be taken as an exogenously given technological datum.

We have now defined and explained the various possibilities for use of the first-period resources. The total of such uses is of course restricted by the available supply; this leads to the first-period *feasibility constraint*:

$$\sum_i C_i + \sum_j I_j + M = Q \qquad (1.2)$$

i.e., total consumption plus total investment (in both risky firms and the riskless opportunity) must equal total supply. Since we shall assume non-satiation (more consumption is always preferred to less) we have written the constraint as a strict equality.

1.5. We now turn to the second period, when the transformation of input into output has been completed. The total amount of income available for distribution to individuals, given that state of the world θ obtains, is then given by

$$W(\theta) \equiv rM + \sum_j X_j(\theta) \qquad (\theta = 1, \ldots, s) \qquad (1.3)$$

We denote by $Y_i(\theta)$ the amount of second-period income to be received by individual i if state of the world θ occurs, altogether ms numbers. For each state of the world, these must satisfy the second-period feasibility constraints

$$\sum_i Y_i(\theta) = W(\theta) \qquad (\theta = 1, \ldots, s) \qquad (1.4)$$

The complete specification of a feasible allocation thus amounts to determining $m + n + 1 + ms$ numbers $\{C_i, I_j, M, Y_i(\theta)\}$ satisfying the $s + 1$ feasibility constraints (1.2) and (1.4), where the $W(\theta)$ are defined by (1.3) and the $X_j(\theta)$ by (1.1).

In Figure 1-1, the single arrows represent simple source-use relationships, while the double arrows connecting first- and second-period variables represent transformations: the input I_j is transformed into the second-period random output $X_j(\theta)$, while the input M to the riskless industry is transformed into the certain output rM.

1.6. So far we have said nothing on how a particular allocation is brought about, nor on how a given allocation can be evaluated in terms of desirability. As for the former, we shall naturally be particularly concerned with allocations that are effected through competitive trading of various kinds of financial claims. First, however, we shall examine the concept of efficiency (or Pareto optimality) and the role of that concept as a criterion for social welfare.

2

The Concept of Efficiency

2.1. It is useful to start the analysis of efficiency of financial markets with a brief review of the classical theory of efficiency of a commodity exchange market under certainty. This will help to clarify basic concepts and establish a certain analytical apparatus.

Consider an economy with m individuals and n commodities, and let x_{ij} be the amount of commodity j received by individual i. The total supply of each commodity is fixed, so that any allocation must satisfy the feasibility constraints

$$\sum_i x_{ij} = v_j \qquad (j = 1, \ldots, n) \tag{2.1}$$

where v_j is the given supply of commodity j.

Each individual is assumed to have a preference ordering over commodity combinations allocated to him which can be represented by a strictly increasing, concave utility function

$$U_i = f_i(x_{i1}, \ldots, x_{in})$$

Now consider two allocations $\{x_{ij}^1\}$ and $\{x_{ij}^2\}$ with corresponding utility levels $\{U_i^1\}$ and $\{U_i^2\}$. We say that the allocation $\{x_{ij}^1\}$ *dominates* the allocation $\{x_{ij}^2\}$ if $U_i^1 \geq U_i^2$ for all i and $U_i^1 > U_i^2$ for at least one i. Thus, an allocation dominates another if it gives one or more individuals a higher utility level without giving any individual a lower utility level. A reasonable condition to impose on an allocation is that it should not be dominated by another allocation; otherwise the allocation would represent an inefficient use of the given resources. This leads us to require that an allocation be efficient, or Pareto-optimal, in the sense that there should exist no other feasible allocation that dominates it.

The concept of Pareto-optimality is illustrated in Figure 2-1 for a case involving two individuals. When the utility functions are concave (i.e., represented by indifference curves that are convex to the origin), the set of feasible allocations generates a set of utility levels (U_1, U_2) that is convex (the shaded area). Any point inside this set, such as P, is inefficient, since it is possible to find another allocation that is preferred by both individuals. Along the northeast boundary of the set, however, no such reallocation is possible; any movement from a point such as Q must lead to a less preferred position for at least one of the individuals.

7

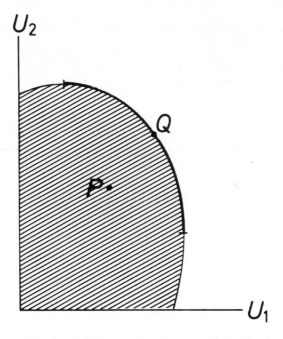

Figure 2-1. Pareto-Optimality for Two Individuals.

Algebraically, we can formulate the condition of Pareto-optimality as follows. Let the allocation x_{ij} be changed to $x_{ij} + dx_{ij}$. Then the change in individual is utility is

$$dU_i = \sum_j f_{ij}\, dx_{ij} \qquad (i = 1, \ldots, m)$$

where f_{ij} denotes the partial derivative $\partial f_i/\partial x_{ij}$. Any such reallocation must clearly satisfy the feasibility constraints, i.e., we must have

$$\sum_i dx_{ij} = 0 \qquad (j = 1, \ldots, n) \qquad (2.2)$$

The allocation x_{ij} is then Pareto-optimal if and only if the dU_i are not all positive (or if they are all zero).

The following theorem is useful in determining the set of Pareto-optimal allocations.

Theorem. An allocation is Pareto-optimal if and only if

$$k_i f_{ij} = f_{1j} \qquad (i = 1, \ldots, m; \quad j = 1, \ldots, n) \qquad (2.3)$$

where $k_1 = 1$ and $k_2, \ldots, k_m$ are arbitrary nonnegative constants.

The theorem is a special case of the Kuhn-Tucker theorem, and can also be proved directly in a simple manner. We shall indicate the ideas behind the proof, following Borch [1].

Let us change the allocation from x_{ij} to $x_{ij} + dx_{ij}$. If the conditions (2.3) are fulfilled, we have

$$k_i dU_i = \sum_j f_{1j} dx_{ij}$$

and hence, in view of (2.2)

$$\sum_i k_i dU_i = \sum_i \sum_j f_{1j} dx_{ij} = \sum_j f_{1j} \sum_i dx_{ij} = 0$$

But with the $k_i > 0$, this implies that the dU_i cannot all be of the same sign (unless they are all zero).

To demonstrate the necessity of the conditions, let $dx_{ij} = 0$ for $i > 2, j > 2$. We must then have

$$dx_{21} = -dx_{11}, \quad dx_{22} = -dx_{12}$$

The changes in utility are

$$dU_1 = f_{11} dx_{11} + f_{12} dx_{12}$$
$$dU_2 = -(f_{21} dx_{11} + f_{22} dx_{12})$$

When the allocation is Pareto-optimal, the product of the utility changes must be nonpositive, hence

$$A \equiv (f_{11} dx_{11} + f_{12} dx_{12})(f_{21} dx_{11} + f_{22} dx_{12}) \geq 0$$

By multiplying out and completing the square, we find that this can be written

$$A = f_{11} f_{21} \left[dx_{11} + \frac{f_{11} f_{22} + f_{12} f_{21}}{2 f_{11} f_{21}} dx_{12} \right]^2$$

$$- \frac{(f_{11} f_{22} - f_{12} f_{21})^2}{4 f_{11} f_{21}} (dx_{12})^2 \geq 0$$

Now, necessary and sufficient conditions for this inequality to be satisfied are that $f_{11} f_{21} \geq 0$ and $(f_{11} f_{22} - f_{12} f_{21})^2 \leq 0$, but this latter inequality can hold only if

$$\frac{f_{11}}{f_{21}} = \frac{f_{12}}{f_{22}}$$

i.e., when conditions (2.3) are fulfilled. Hence, if follows that (2.3) is also a necessary condition for Pareto-optimality.

If the utility functions are concave (i.e., have convex indifferences curves), the conditions (2.3) also represent conditions for a maximum of $\sum_i k_i U_i$ subject to the market clearing conditions. For by forming the Lagrangean

$$L = \sum_i k_i U_i + \sum_j \lambda_j \left(v_j - \sum_i x_{ij} \right)$$

we get the first-order conditions for a maximum

$$\frac{\partial L}{\partial x_{ij}} = k_i f_{ij} - \lambda_j = 0 \qquad (i = 1, \ldots, m; \quad j = 1, \ldots, n)$$

which are identical with (2.3). Thus, the theorem might just as well have said that an allocation is Pareto-optimal if and only if it maximizes a positively weighted sum of individual utilities. The theorem can then easily be interpreted geometrically: Any point along the northeast boundary of the feasible set of Figure 2-1 represents the maximum of a positively weighted sum $U_1 + kU_2$; by letting k vary we obtain the set of all Pareto-optimal allocations.

2.2. One of the central results of classical equilibrium theory is that if our persons organize the commodity allocation by means of trading at prices p_j that clear all markets, then the resulting allocation is Pareto-optimal. Conversely, any Pareto-optimal allocation can be obtained by specifying an initial allocation y_{ij} and a set of prices p_j and letting people trade at these prices.

In a competitive market, the demand of person i is determined by his attempt to maximize $U_i = f_i(x_{i1}, \ldots, x_{in})$ subject to his budget condition

$$\sum_j p_j x_{ij} = \sum_j p_j y_{ij}$$

The solution to this problem is given by the well-known conditions

$$f_{ij} = \lambda_i p_j \qquad (i = 1, \ldots, m; \qquad j = 1, \ldots, n)$$

where λ_i is a Lagrangean multiplier. These conditions can be written

$$\frac{\lambda_1}{\lambda_i} f_{ij} = f_{1j}$$

and are then seen to be identical with conditions (2.3). Hence the market allocation is Pareto-optimal. This result provides the basic theoretical justification for a competitive market economy.

2.3. Let us now return to our model of allocation of consumption and investment under uncertainty. Here we first assume that each individual has a (subjective) probability distribution $f_i(\theta)$ over states of the world, i.e., $f_i(\theta)$ is the probability that individual i attaches to the possibility of state of the world occuring. Second, we assume that each individual has a preference ordering over combinations of first-period consumption C_i and probability distributions for second-period income $Y_i(\theta)$ that can be represented in terms of expected utility as

$$U_i = \sum_{\theta} u_i(C_i, Y_i(\theta)) f_i(\theta) \qquad (2.4)$$

where u_i is the individual's cardinal (von Neumann-Morgenstern) utility function, uniquely determined up to a positive linear (or affine) transformation. This function is assumed to be strictly increasing and strictly concave, thus representing risk aversion with respect to a second-period income. Note that the formulation (2.4) excludes so-called "state contingent utilities": a dollar is a dollar regardless of the particular state of the world in which it is received.

While at it, we also introduce the expectation operator $\mathscr{E}_i$ with respect to the probability distribution $f_i(\theta)$; thus (2.4) can be written more compactly as

$$U_i = \mathscr{E}_i[u_i(C_i, Y_i)] \qquad (2.5)$$

In expressions using the expectation operator, we shall usually suppress the functional dependence of random variables on θ.

Just as in the commodity exchange case, we define Pareto-optimality as nondominance, only here in terms of expected utility. A Pareto-optimal allocation is then correspondingly one which for some set of nonnegative numbers k_i ($i = 1, \ldots, m$) maximizes the weighted sum $\Sigma k_i U_i$ subject to the feasibility constraints (1.2) and (1.4).

To characterize the Pareto-optimal allocations, we form the Lagrangean

$$L = \sum_i k_i U_i + \mu \left(Q - \sum_i C_i - \sum_j I_j - M \right)$$

$$+ \sum_{\theta} \beta(\theta) \left[rM + \sum_j X_j(\theta) - \sum_i Y_i(\theta) \right]$$

where μ is the Lagrange multiplier associated with (1.2) and $\beta(\theta)$ the multiplier associated with θth of the constraints (1.4). The first-order conditions for a maximum are then

$$\frac{\partial L}{\partial C_i} = k_i \sum_{\theta} u_{iC}(C_i, Y_i(\theta)) f_i(\theta) - \mu = 0 \qquad (2.6)$$

$$\frac{\partial L}{\partial I_j} = -\mu + \sum_{\theta} \beta(\theta) \phi_j'(I_j, \theta) = 0 \qquad (2.7)$$

$$\frac{\partial L}{\partial M} = -\mu + r\sum_{\theta}\beta(\theta) = 0 \tag{2.8}$$

$$\frac{\partial L}{\partial Y_i(\theta)} = k_i u_{iY}(C_i, Y_i(\theta))f_i(\theta) - \beta(\theta) = 0 \tag{2.9}$$

Here u_{iC} and u_{iY} denote partial derivatives of u_i with respect to first- and second-period income, respectively, and

$$\phi_j'(I_j, \theta) = \frac{dX_j(\theta)}{dI_j} = \frac{\partial}{\partial I_j}\phi_j(I_j, \theta)$$

As far as the interpretation of equations (2.6) through (2.9) is concerned, we first note that from (2.9)

$$k_i u_{iY}(C_i, Y_i(\theta))f_i(\theta) = u_{1Y}(C_1, Y_1(\theta))f_1(\theta)$$

for every i and θ. Thus the allocation must be such that for any two individuals, the marginal utilities of second-period income, weighted by their probability of occurrence, stand in the same proportion to each other in all states of the world. This basically represents conditions on the allocation of second-period income among individuals.

From (2.6) we have

$$\sum_{\theta} u_{iC}(C_i, Y_i(\theta))f_i(\theta) = \mu/k_i$$

or, more compactly

$$\mathscr{E}_i[u_{iC}(C_i, Y_i)] = \mu/k_i \tag{2.10}$$

Furthermore, substituting from (2.9), $\beta(\theta) = k_i u_{iY}(C_i, Y_i(\theta))f_i(\theta)$ into (2.7) and (2.8) we obtain, respectively,

$$\mathscr{E}_i[u_{iY}(C_i, Y_i)\phi_j'(I_j, \theta)] = \mu/k_i \tag{2.11}$$

$$r\mathscr{E}_i[u_{iY}(C_i, Y_i)] = \mu/k_i \tag{2.12}$$

Thus the left hand sides of all three sets of equations (2.10) through (2.12) must be equal.

Equating (2.10) and (2.12), we have

$$\mathscr{E}_i[u_{iC}(C_i, Y_i)] = r\mathscr{E}_i[u_{iY}(C_i, Y_i)]$$

This represents conditions on the relationships between first- and second-period income and is the generalization to the case of uncertainty of the Fisherian rule of intertemporal allocation: equality between the certainty equivalent marginal rate of time preference with one plus the interest rate; this certainty equivalent marginal rate of time preference being expressed in terms of *expected* marginal utilities.

Finally, equating (2.11) and (2.12), we obtain

$$\mathscr{E}_i\{u_{iY}(C_i,\ Y_i)[\phi_j'(I_j,\ \theta) - r]\} = 0$$

for every i and j. This can be interpreted as conditions on the allocation of investment capital among risky firms and the riskless opportunity: $\phi_j' - r$ is the (random) net return on the last dollar invested in risky firm j; $u_{iY}(\phi_j' - r)$ is then the (random) second-period utility increment from this investment; the allocation must thus be such that for every firm and every individual the expectation of this utility increment is equal to zero.

In the remainder of the book we shall be concerned with the allocations that result from various kinds of market trading and their efficiency properties.

References

1. Borch, K.H., "Economics and Game Theory," *Swedish Journal of Economics*, 1967, pp. 215-228.

**Part II
Complete Markets**

Introduction

So far, we have looked at the utilization of first-period resources and the allocation of second-period income purely from a central planner's point of view. We now wish to examine the equilibrium allocation in a private ownership economy where compensation from firms for providing investment capital, and the subsequent distribution of output among individuals is effected by means of securities issued by firms and traded in organized, competitive markets.

The concept of equilibrium is essentially static, describing a situation where demand is equal to supply for all securities, so that realized transactions are equal to the planned ones for all economic agents. We shall not discuss in any detail the dynamics of the process by which such an equilibrium position is actually attained. As an aid to intuition, however, it may be useful to think in terms of a process of *recontracting*, possibly aided by a "market manager." The market manager announces a set of prices; firms can then calculate what they consider optimal security issues and individuals can calculate what they consider optimal consumption levels and security purchases. These (tentative) plans are transmitted to the market manager; he then sums up and compares demand with supply for every security; if these are equal, the transactions will be effected; otherwise a new set of prices is announced and the process repeated until equilibrium is reached.

In practice, firms can issue a variety of securities with different yield characteristics: bonds of varying maturities, common stock, preferred stock, convertible bonds and other kinds of hybrid securities are some examples. The most prevalent, of course, are *bonds*, which (barring default) give a fixed amount of output per unit of input, and *common stock*, giving a fixed fraction of output net of payment to bondholders.

As far as problems of efficiency are concerned, an important consideration is the *number* of different securities available as compared to the number of distinct states of the world. To see what is involved, consider a simple example with three states of the world and two securities with second-period payments as given in Table II-1. For concreteness, we may think of these securities as the common stock of Company 1 and Company 2, respectively. These are assumed to be the only securities available in the economy. It is useful to think of such securities as representing *vectors* of second-period output across states of the world, and in the same way to think of an individual's uncertain income, $Y_i(\theta)$, as a vector with elements $Y_i(1)$, $Y_i(2)$, ..., $Y_i(s)$ and thus geometrically as a point in an s-dimensional income space. The income from a *portfolio* of securities then represent a linear combination of the corresponding output vectors.

Table II-1
Example Situation: Three States of the World and Two Securities

	State of the World		
	1	*2*	*3*
Security 1	100	150	150
Security 2	0	100	250

Thus, if in our example individual i holds a fraction z_{i1} of the outstanding shares of Company 1 and a fraction z_{i2} of the shares of Company 2, his second-period income is given by the linear combination

$$\begin{bmatrix} Y_i(1) \\ Y_i(2) \\ Y_i(3) \end{bmatrix} = \begin{bmatrix} 100 \\ 150 \\ 150 \end{bmatrix} z_{i1} + \begin{bmatrix} 0 \\ 100 \\ 250 \end{bmatrix} z_{i2}$$

Quite generally, the individual's portfolio selection problem can be characterized as one of finding a preferred point in the s-dimensional income space. The important point now, however, is that when there are fewer securities available than there are states of the world, the individual's choice among income vectors is *restricted to a subspace of the complete s-dimensional income space*. In the example, he is restricted to a two-dimensional linear subspace (a plane) in the three-dimensional income space. Thus, while the income vector (30, 55, 70) is obtainable (by choosing $z_{i1} = 0.3$, $z_{i2} = 0.10$), the vector (30, 55, 80) is not.

Of course, in a market setting the individual would also be restricted by a budget condition, but here we want to concentrate on the structural restriction imposed on the set of attainable income vectors by an insufficient number of securities to span the complete income space. It is important to realize that the "elementary commodities" to be allocated among individuals in such a market are not really stocks or bonds or similar securities, but rather claims to income in different states of the world. At least on an abstract level we could conceive of a market where such claims were traded directly. We would then have a number of securities, one for each state of the world, promising to pay one unit of money if that particular state occured, and nothing otherwise. Such securities are referred to as *state contingent claims*, or *Arrow-Debreu securities*. Such a market would represent an ideal way of organizing the allocation of second-period income, since with these securities individuals would have complete freedom, subject only to their budget constraints, to obtain a preferred distribution of income in different states of the world. If, on the other hand, we have an incomplete set of securities, then we shall see that the market allocation will be Pareto-optimal only under rather restrictive conditions. First, however, let us turn to the analysis of a market with a complete set of state contingent claims.

3

State Contingent Claims

3.1. Let the price of a "state-θ-security," i.e., a security that pays one unit of output if state of the world θ occurs, be $\pi(\theta)$. Both firms, in making their investment decisions, and individuals, in making their consumption-portfolio decisions, are assumed to take these prices as given data.

Consider first the behavior of risky firm j with the production function $X_j(\theta) = \phi_j(I_j, \theta)$. The number of state-$\theta$-securities that the firm can issue is of course precisely equal to $X_j(\theta)$; hence, observing the prices $\pi(\theta)$ in the market, the firm can calculate the total proceeds from its sale of securities as $\Sigma_\theta \pi(\theta) X_j(\theta)$. After using the amount I_j for its investment, the excess cash, which we may call the firm's profits, is

$$\Pi_j = \sum_\theta \pi(\theta) X_j(\theta) - I_j$$

This amount is immediately distributed to the firm's owners according to their initial ownership in the firm. Note that this "dividend" is paid in the first period and is therefore available to the owners for first-period consumption or securities purchases. In the second period, when the state of the world has become known, the firm will simply pay off the corresponding securities and have no cash left. Note also that the profits Π_j is nonrandom and requires no probability calculations on the part of the firm; probabilities are only indirectly reflected in the equilibrium prices $\pi(\theta)$.

To illustrate, suppose a firm has a choice between two investment plans A and B with investment levels and second-period returns in two states of the world as shown in Table 3-1. Assume further that the security prices ruling in the market are $\pi(1) = 0.50$, $\pi(2) = 0.30$. If the firm adopts plan A, it can sell 2000 state-2-securities, which will bring in $600 and thus give a cash excess of $200. If it adopts plan B, it can sell 500 state-1-securities and 4000 state-2-securities with total proceeds of $1,450 with a profit of $150. Acting in its owners' best interest, the firm should clearly choose plan A. The reader should verify that if the security prices instead had been $\pi(1) = 0.2$, $\pi(2) = 0.7$, the choice would have been reversed, with profits of $1,000 and $1,600 for plan A and B, respectively.

Although we refer to Π_j as the firm's profits, it would be equally appropriate to take Π_j as an expression for the (net) *market value* of the firm. Since $\pi(\theta)$ is the market value of a claim to one unit of output if state θ occurs, $\Sigma_\theta \pi(\theta) X_j(\theta)$ is just the market value of the output vector $X_j(\theta)$,

Table 3-1
Example: Investment Levels and Returns for Two Investment Plans

		State of the World		
Plan	I_j	1	2	Π_j
A	400	0	2000	200
B	1300	500	4000	150

and hence $\Sigma_\theta \pi(\theta)X_j(\theta) - I_j$ the amount that the firm's owners could obtain by selling the firm (before the investment has actually been effected).

In the following we shall assume that $X_j(\theta) = \phi_j(I_j, \theta)$ is a continuous, differentiable, concave function of I_j, and that the firm will select a level of I_j so as to maximize its profits (or market value). This leads to the first-order optimality conditions

$$\frac{d\Pi_j}{dI_j} = \sum_\theta \pi(\theta)\phi_j'(I_j, \theta) - 1 = 0 \qquad (j = 1, \ldots, n) \qquad (3.1)$$

We also assume, of course, that the prices $\pi(\theta)$ and the production function are such that at the solution to (3.1) profits is nonnegative; otherwise the firm would not be in business in the first place.

3.2. We now turn to the behavior of individuals. Their initial resources, which represent exogenously given data, are of two kinds. First, they own given supplies q_i of investment capital, which is to be taken as the dollar value of their holdings of factors of production, or, if we adopt the single-commodity interpretation of the model literally, as the number of physical units of this commodity (bushels of corn, say) that they own. Second, they may have ownership holdings in firms, and therefore receive a share of these firms' profits as explained earlier. Thus, if individual i owns a fraction $\bar{z}_{ij}$ of firm j, the total he receives of such dividends is $\Sigma_j \bar{z}_{ij}\Pi_j$. Altogether, then, the amount that individual i has available for first-period consumption and investment in risky firms or the riskless industry is defined by

$$W_i \equiv q_i + \sum_j \bar{z}_{ij}\Pi_j \qquad (3.2)$$

We refer to this as individual i's *initial wealth*. Note that the value of initial wealth depends both on the security prices $\pi(\theta)$ and the investment levels chosen by firms through its dependence on the Π_j. Thus, firms will have to have announced their investment plans before individuals can make their consumption-investment decisions.

If individual i wishes to obtain a second-period income of $Y_i(\theta)$ if state of the world θ occurs, that is of course precisely the number of state-θ-

securities he has to buy. Thus, $Y_i(\theta)$ represents both the vector of second-period income and the vector of purchases of the different kinds of state contingent claims. The total amount spent on securities is then $\Sigma_\theta \pi(\theta) Y_i(\theta)$, and the individual's *budget constraint* is therefore

$$\sum_\theta \pi(\theta) Y_i(\theta) + C_i = W_i \qquad (i = 1, \ldots, m) \qquad (3.3)$$

where as before C_i is his first-period consumption.

As described in chapter 2, we assume that the individual's preference ordering over combinations of first-period consumption and probability distributions for second-period income can be represented in terms of expected utility as

$$U_i = \sum_\theta u_i(C_i, Y_i(\theta)) f_i(\theta)$$

His decision problem is therefore to select the $s + 1$ variables C_i and $Y_i(\theta)$ so as to maximize U_i subject to his budget constraint (3.3) with W_i and the $\pi(\theta)$ as given data. Forming the Lagrangean

$$L_i = \sum_\theta u_i(C_i, Y_i(\theta)) f_i(\theta) + \lambda_i \left[W_i - \sum_\theta \pi(\theta) Y_i(\theta) - C_i \right]$$

we obtain the first-order maximum conditions

$$\frac{\partial L_i}{\partial Y_i(\theta)} = u_{iY}(C_i, Y_i(\theta)) f_i(\theta) - \lambda_i \pi(\theta) = 0 \qquad (\theta = 1, \ldots, s) \quad (3.4)$$

$$\frac{\partial L_i}{\partial C_i} = \sum_\theta u_{iC}(C_i, Y_i(\theta)) f_i(\theta) - \lambda_i = 0 \qquad (3.5)$$

3.3. The complete general equilibrium model must also include market clearing conditions corresponding to the feasibility constraints (1.2) and (1.4). These must take the form

$$\sum_i C_i + \sum_j I_j + M = \sum_i q_i \qquad (3.6)$$

$$\sum_i Y_i(\theta) = \sum_j X_j(\theta) + rM \qquad (\theta = 1, \ldots, s) \qquad (3.7)$$

Clearly, the sum $\Sigma_i q_i$ is just the total economy-wide supply of initial resources Q defined in chapter 1.

3.4. In all, the model consists of the n equations (3.1), the sm equations (3.4), the m equations (3.5), the (single) equation (3.6) and the s equations (3.7). The variables to be determined by these equations are the n investment levels I_j, the sm income allocations $Y_i(\theta)$, the m first-period consumption levels C_i, the investment M in the riskless industry, and the s security prices $\pi(\theta)$. We assume, of course, that a solution exists, and given the assumption of strictly increasing, concave production and utility functions, the solution is also unique.

We note that because of the constant returns to scale assumption for the riskless industry, there is no condition explicitly determining the optimal level of M. Rather, once the I_j have been determined from (3.1) and the C_i from (3.4) and (3.5), M is determined residually from (3.6).

The model has another interesting property. We notice that it contains exactly as many equations as there are variables to be determined. Now, in "ordinary" general equilibrium models we typically find that one of the market clearing conditions is superfluous, so that only *relative* prices can be determined. This is not immediately evident from the model as specified above. To see what is involved, observe that a portfolio consisting of one of every security would pay one dollar with absolute certainty. The cost of such a package would be $\Sigma_\theta \pi(\theta)$. Now, an investment of the amount $1/r$ in the riskless industry would also return one dollar with certainty. We would obviously feel rather uncomfortable if the model did not determine the $\pi(\theta)$ such that

$$\sum_\theta \pi(\theta) = \frac{1}{r} \qquad (3.8)$$

There are two ways of going about this. We can either explicitly require the normalization (3.8); in that case it is fairly straightforward to show that one of the market clearing conditions is superfluous so that such a normalization imposes no inconsistency on the model. The other (and more interesting) possibility is to take the market clearing conditions as independent and then show that the model implies the above normalization of prices. Following this approach, we first sum the budget equations (3.3) (with W_i substituted from (3.2)) over i:

$$\sum_i \sum_\theta \pi(\theta) Y_i(\theta) + \sum_i C_i = \sum_i q_i + \sum_i \sum_j \bar{z}_{ij} \Pi_j \qquad (3.9)$$

Using (3.7) and the definition of Π_j we have here

$$\sum_i \sum_\theta \pi(\theta) Y_i(\theta) = \sum_\theta \pi(\theta) \sum_i Y_i(\theta)$$

$$= \sum_\theta \pi(\theta) \left[\sum_j X_j(\theta) + rM \right]$$

$$= \sum_j \sum_\theta \pi(\theta) X_j(\theta) + rM \sum_\theta \pi(\theta)$$

$$= \sum_j (\Pi_j + I_j) + rM \sum_\theta \pi(\theta)$$

Furthermore, since by definition the initial ownership of firms must have been such that

$$\sum_i \bar{z}_{ij} = 1 \qquad (j = 1, \ldots, n)$$

we have

$$\sum_i \sum_j \bar{z}_{ij} \Pi_j = \sum_j \Pi_j \sum_i \bar{z}_{ij} = \sum_j \Pi_j$$

Substituting into (3.9), the term $\Sigma_j \Pi_j$ drops out on both sides, and we are left with

$$\sum_j I_j + rM \sum_\theta \pi(\theta) + \sum_i C_i = \sum_i q_i$$

or

$$rM \sum_\theta \pi(\theta) = \sum_i q_i - \sum_i C_i - \sum_j I_j$$

But from (3.6) the right hand side equals M, hence (3.8) follows.

3.5. We now show that the market allocation described above represents a Pareto optimum. We do this by showing that no feasible reallocation in the neighborhood of the equilibrium market allocation can be preferred by all individuals. Thus, consider a reallocation $\{dC_i, dI_j, dM, dY_i(\theta)\}$; in order to be feasible, this must satisfy

$$\sum_i dC_i + \sum_j dI_j + dM = 0 \qquad (3.10)$$

$$\sum_i dY_i(\theta) = \sum_j dX_j(\theta) + rdM \qquad (3.11)$$

where $dX_j(\theta) = \phi_j'(I_j, \theta)dI_j$.

The changes in expected utilities

$$U_i = \sum_\theta u_i(C_i, Y_i(\theta))f_i(\theta)$$

caused by the reallocation are

$$dU_i = \sum_\theta [u_{iC}(C_i, Y_i(\theta))dC_i + u_{iY}(C_i, Y_i(\theta))dY_i(\theta)]f_i(\theta)$$

$$= \left[\sum_\theta u_{iC}(C_i, Y_i(\theta))f_i(\theta)\right]dC_i$$

$$+ \sum_\theta u_{iY}(C_i, Y_i(\theta))f_i(\theta)dY_i(\theta)$$

From (3.5) we have

$$\sum_{\theta} u_{iC}(C_i,\ Y_i(\theta))f_i(\theta) = \lambda_i$$

and from (3.4)

$$u_{iY}(C_i,\ Y_i(\theta))f_i(\theta) = \lambda_i \pi(\theta)$$

implying

$$\sum_{\theta} u_{iY}(C_i,\ Y_i(\theta))f_i(\theta)dY_i(\theta) = \lambda_i \sum_{\theta} \pi(\theta)dY_i(\theta)$$

Accordingly, changes in expected utility in the neighborhood of the market equilibrium are such that

$$dU_i = \lambda_i dC_i + \lambda_i \sum_{\theta} \pi(\theta)d Y_i(\theta)$$

or

$$\frac{1}{\lambda_i}dU_i = dC_i + \sum_{\theta} \pi(\theta)dY_i(\theta)$$

Summing over i gives

$$\sum_i \frac{1}{\lambda_i}dU_i = \sum_i dC_i + \sum_i \sum_{\theta} \pi(\theta)dY_i(\theta)$$

$$= \sum_i dC_i + \sum_{\theta} \pi(\theta)\sum_i dY_i(\theta)$$

$$= \sum_i dC_i + \sum_{\theta} \pi(\theta)\left[\sum_j dX_j(\theta) + rdM\right]$$

$$= \sum_i dC_i + \sum_{\theta} \pi(\theta)\left[\sum_j \phi_j'(I_j,\ \theta)dI_j + rdM\right]$$

$$= \sum_i dC_i + \sum_j \sum_{\theta} \pi(\theta)\phi_j'(I_j,\ \theta)dI_j + rdM \sum_{\theta} \pi(\theta)$$

$$= \sum_i dC_i + \sum_j dI_j + dM$$

where we have used successively, (3.11), (3.1), and (3.8). But from (3.10), the right hand side equals zero; hence

$$\sum_i \frac{1}{\lambda_i}dU_i = 0$$

Since the Lagrange multipliers λ_i in equilibrium equal the marginal expected utilities of initial wealth, they are (by the assumption of nonsatiation) positive; this implies that the dU_i cannot all be positive, and the Pareto-optimality of the market allocation follows.

3.6. Although of a certain theoretical interest, it may be argued that a market for state contingent claims is empirically irrelevant, since in the real world a complete set of state contingent claims in pure form does not exist. As indicated earlier, this in itself is not so important as the requirement that the number of securities be as large as the number of states of the world. To examine this, we shall formulate a model of a market for bonds and common stock.

4

Complete Stock Markets

4.1. To keep things simple at the present stage, assume that all risky firms are wholly equity financed, so that outstanding bonds represent either claims on the riskless industry or interpersonal lending/borrowing, also assumed riskless. Denote by $\bar{n}_j$ the number of shares in Company j initially outstanding; these are given data. Of these, individual i initially owns the fraction $\bar{z}_{ij}$, so that the number of shares he owns is $\bar{n}_{ij} = \bar{z}_{ij}\bar{n}_j$. Since

$$\sum_i \bar{z}_{ij} = 1$$

we obviously also have

$$\sum_i \bar{n}_{ij} = \bar{n}_j$$

To finance its investment, the firm will have to issue additional shares; we denote the total number of shares outstanding after the issue by n_j, so that the new issue itself consists of $n_j - \bar{n}_j$ shares. Further, let p_j be the market value of *all* outstanding shares (the market value of the firm), so that the market price per share—both old and new—is p_j/n_j. To obtain an investment capital in the amount I_j, the firm thus has to sell shares such that

$$\frac{p_j}{n_j}(n_j - \bar{n}_j) = I_j$$

i.e., an increase to

$$n_j = \frac{p_j\bar{n}_j}{p_j - I_j} \tag{4.1}$$

Individuals' initial resources include, in addition to their shareholdings, given supplies q_i of investment capital. The initial wealth of individual i is thus given by

$$W_i \equiv q_i + \sum_j \bar{n}_{ij}\frac{p_j}{n_j} \tag{4.2}$$

Let m_i be individual i's investment in riskless bonds (net riskless lending), and n_{ij} the number of shares in firm j that he buys. His budget constraint is then

29

$$C_i + m_i + \sum_j n_{ij} \frac{p_j}{n_j} = W_i \tag{4.3}$$

and his second-period income correspondingly

$$Y_i(\theta) = rm_i + \sum_j \frac{n_{ij}}{n_j} X_j(\theta) \tag{4.4}$$

since n_{ij}/n_j is the fraction of firm j's output claimed by individual i and rm_i the return on his bonds.

Finally, the allocation of shares must satisfy the market clearing conditions

$$\sum_i n_{ij} = n_j \qquad (j = 1, \ldots, n) \tag{4.5}$$

Note that these conditions ensure that the feasibility conditions (1.2) and (1.4) are satisfied. For taking the budget conditions

$$C_i + m_i + \sum_j n_{ij} \frac{p_j}{n_j} = q_i + \sum_j \bar{n}_{ij} \frac{p_j}{n_j}$$

and summing over i gives

$$\sum_i C_i + \sum_i m_i + \sum_i \sum_j n_{ij} \frac{p_j}{n_j} = \sum_i q_i + \sum_i \sum_j \bar{n}_{ij} \frac{p_j}{n_j}$$

Here, $\Sigma_i m_i = M$ and $\Sigma_i q_i = Q$, hence

$$\sum_i C_i + M + \sum_j \frac{p_j}{n_j} \sum_i n_{ij} = Q + \sum_j \frac{p_j}{n_j} \sum_i \bar{n}_{ij}$$

or, using (4.5),

$$\sum_i C_i + M + \sum_j p_j = Q + \sum_j \frac{p_j \bar{n}_j}{n_j}$$

But from (4.1), $p_j \bar{n}_j / n_j = p_j - I$, so that

$$\sum_i C_i + M + \sum_j p_j = Q + \sum_j (p_j - I_j)$$

The terms $\Sigma_j p_j$ on both sides cancel, and (1.2) then follows. Similarly, summing the expression (4.4) for second-period income over i gives

$$\sum_i Y_i(\theta) = r \sum_i m_i + \sum_i \sum_j \frac{n_{ij}}{n_j} X_j(\theta)$$

$$= rM + \sum_j \frac{X_j(\theta)}{n_j} \sum_i n_{ij}$$

$$= rM + \sum_j X_j(\theta)$$

so that also (1.4) are satisfied.

Table 4-1
Numerical Example for Feasibility Relationships

	Ind. 1	Ind. 2	Totals
Investment capital	$q_1 = 500$	$q_2 = 300$	$Q = 800$
Shares in firm 1	$\bar{n}_{11} = 80$	$\bar{n}_{21} = 120$	$\bar{n}_1 = 200$
Shares in firm 2	$\bar{n}_{12} = 100$	$\bar{n}_{22} = 0$	$\bar{n}_2 = 100$

Table 4-2
Optimal Portfolios

	Ind. 1	Ind. 2
Shares in firm 1	$n_{11} = 250$	$n_{21} = 250$
Shares in firm 2	$n_{12} = 150$	$n_{22} = 50$

4.2. To illustrate the relationships above, consider a numerical example involving two firms and two individuals with initial resources as in Table 4-1. Suppose that the equilibrium values of the firms are $p_1 = 500$, $p_2 = 400$, and that the firms somehow have chosen the investment levels $I_1 = 300$, $I_2 = 200$. The number of shares outstanding will then have to be increased to

$$n_1 = \frac{500 \cdot 200}{500 - 300} = 500$$

i.e., 300 new shares at \$1 per share, and

$$n_2 = \frac{400 \cdot 100}{400 - 200} = 200$$

i.e., 100 new shares at \$2 per share. The individuals can then calculate the value of their holdings as

$$W_1 = 500 + 80 \cdot 1 + 100 \cdot 2 = 780$$

and

$$W_2 = 300 + 120 \cdot 1 + 0 \cdot 2 = 420$$

Given these wealth levels and the second-period output vectors $X_j(\theta)$ corresponding to the investment levels I_j, suppose that the optimal portfolios are as shown in Table 4-2. The cost of these shares will be \$550 for individual 1 and hence his riskless investment \$230; for individual 2 and the corresponding figures are \$350 and \$70, respectively. Thus, investment in the riskless industry is $300 (we have here disregarded first-period consumption). With the investment levels $I_1 = 300$ and $I_2 = 200$ in the risky firms, the total amount of investment is therefore $800, which is precisely the total amount of investment capital that was available.

4.3. So far we have said nothing about how firms actually decide on their investment levels and corresponding share issues, nor on how individuals make their consumption/portfolio decisions. This brings us back to the matter of the number of different securities as compared with the number of different states of the world, and it should by now be fairly easy to see why. The idea is the following: even though prices for state contingent claims are not explicitly quoted in a stock market, when such a market has a sufficient number of different securities available, each with a given market value, then it is possible to infer a set of *imputed* prices for state contingent claims. If then firms and individuals behave as if such imputed prices were computed and used for decision making purposes in the way described in chapter 3, the resulting allocation will be Pareto-optimal. Thus it is in this case possible to establish the Pareto-optimality of an allocation effected by a market for stocks and bonds by invoking an imaginary shadow market with a complete set of state contingent claims. We shall try to explain these ideas in more detail.

Consider again the numerical example of a stock market allocation. Suppose that there are three states of the world and that with the given investment levels second-period output of the two firms will be as shown in Table 4-3. Suppose further that the return on riskless investment is 1.25, i.e., an interest rate of 25%, and assume finally that the market values of the shares of the two firms are $p_1 = 500$ and $p_2 = 400$.

Given these return distributions and share values, we can infer what a set of prices $\pi(\theta)$ for state contingent claims must be that will sustain these share values. By this we mean that they are such that for every firm they generate a value of its output that is just equal to the (given) market value of its shares. Such a set of prices are therefore a solution to the linear equations

$$\left. \begin{array}{l} \Sigma_\theta \pi(\theta) X_j(\theta) = p_j \quad (j = 1, \ldots, n) \\[2mm] \Sigma_\theta \pi(\theta) = 1/r \end{array} \right\} \tag{4.6}$$

In our example, these equations take the form

$$500\pi(1) + 700\pi(2) + 900\pi(3) = 500$$

$$800\pi(2) + 1600\pi(3) = 400$$

$$\pi(1) + \pi(2) + \pi(3) = 0.8$$

and the reader can verify that the solution is given by

Table 4-3
Second-Period Output

	State		
	1	*2*	*3*
$X_1(\theta)$	500	700	900
$X_2(\theta)$	0	800	1600

Table 4-4
Solution for Purchases of State Contingent Claims

	State			*Total*
	1	*2*	*3*	*cost*
Ind. 1	550	1230	1910	780
Ind. 2	325	645	965	420
Sum	875	1875	2875	1200

$$\pi(1) = 0.40; \qquad \pi(2) = 0.30; \qquad \pi(3) = 0.10$$

Using the prices $\pi(\theta)$ so computed, individuals can now from (3.2) calculate their initial wealth. Thus, the profits Π_j of the two firms are in our case

$$\Pi_1 = 500 \cdot 0.40 + 700 \cdot 0.30 + \ 900 \cdot 0.10 - 300 = 200$$

$$\Pi_2 = \qquad\qquad\quad 800 \cdot 0.30 + 1600 \cdot 0.10 - 200 = 200$$

Individual 1's initial ownership of the two firms was $z_{11} = 0.4$, $z_{12} = 1.0$ and his initial wealth accordingly

$$W_1 = 500 + 0.4 \cdot 200 + 1.0 \cdot 200 = 780$$

similarly, individual 2's initial wealth is computed as

$$W_2 = 300 + 0.6 \cdot 200 = 420$$

Next, individuals can use (3.3) through (3.5) to determine their fictitious purchases of state contingent claims. Suppose that the utility functions and probability distributions are such that these solutions are given by the vectors shown in Table 4-4. The final step would then be to convert the solution in terms of state contingent claims into a solution in terms of share- and bondholdings. This conversion clearly consists in finding a solution for m_i and the $z_{ij} \equiv n_{ij}/n_j$ to the linear equations (4.14)

$$rm_i + \sum_j z_{ij}X_j(\theta) = Y_i(\theta) \qquad (\theta = 1, \ldots, s)$$

For individual 1 in our example, these equations take the form

$$1.25m_1 + 500z_{11} \qquad\qquad = 550$$
$$1.25m_1 + 700z_{11} + 800z_{12} = 1230$$
$$1.25m_1 + 900z_{11} + 1600z_{12} = 1910$$

with the solution

$$m_1 = 200; \qquad z_{11} = 0.6; \qquad z_{12} = 0.7$$

The cost of this portfolio, in terms of the given share prices, is computed as

$$200 + 0.6 \cdot 500 + 0.7 \cdot 400 = 780$$

The reader can verify that individual 2's equation system has the solution

$$m_2 = 100; \qquad z_{21} = 0.4; \qquad z_{22} = 0.3$$

with a total cost of 420.

We see that the solution we have just derived is the same as the stock/bond allocation that we earlier simply assumed as given. What we have done now, however, is to demonstrate how the optimality conditions (3.3) through (3.5)—which are formulated in terms of state contingent claims and their prices—can be used to characterize optimal portfolios of stocks and bonds. Furthermore, as evidenced by our numerical example, if the budget conditions for state contingent claims are satisfied, then so will the budget conditions for stocks and bonds. To see this in the general case, start with the budget condition for state contingent claims:

$$\sum_\theta \pi(\theta)Y_i(\theta) = q_i + \sum_j \bar{z}_{ij}\Pi_j$$

Using (4.4) and (4.6), the left hand side can be written

$$\sum_\theta \pi(\theta)Y_i(\theta) = \sum_\theta \pi(\theta)\left[rm_i + \sum_j z_{ij}X_j(\theta)\right]$$

$$= rm_i\sum_\theta \pi(\theta) + \sum_\theta\sum_j \pi(\theta)z_{ij}X_j(\theta)$$

$$= m_i + \sum_j z_{ij}\sum_\theta \pi(\theta)X_j(\theta)$$

$$= m_i + \sum_j z_{ij}p_j$$

which is precisely the expenditure on stocks and bonds. As for the right hand side, we have, using the definition of Π_j and then (4.6) and (4.1)

$$q_i + \sum_j \bar{z}_{ij}\Pi_j = q_i + \sum_j \bar{z}_{ij}\left[\sum_\theta \pi(\theta)X_j(\theta) - I_j\right]$$

$$= q_i + \sum_j \bar{z}_{ij}(p_j - I_j)$$

$$= q_i + \sum_j \bar{n}_{ij}\frac{p_j - I_j}{\bar{n}_j}$$

$$= q_i + \sum_j \bar{n}_{ij}\frac{p_j}{n_j}$$

which is the definition of initial wealth in a stock/bond market. What this means is that individuals' opportunity sets for second-period income are the same in a market for stocks and bonds as in a market for state contingent claims. Consequently, if individuals did in fact go through the process as described, the resulting stock/bond allocation would entail second-period income vectors $Y_i(\theta)$ identical with those obtained under a regime of state contingent claims.

4.4. So far we have only described how individuals, given the investment decisions of firms, can determine portfolios consisting of stocks and bonds that nevertheless satisfy the optimality conditions (3.3) through (3.5); we have left open the question of how firms can arrive at what they consider optimal investment decisions. It is clear, however, that *if* firms somehow have chosen investment levels that satisfy conditions (3.1) (with the $\pi(\theta)$ determined by (4.6)), then the resulting stock market allocation represents a Pareto optimum.

The remaining problem, then, is whether in a stock market setting it is possible for firms to calculate investment levels that satisfy (3.1). In general, no simple solution to this problem would seem to suggest itself: a set of prices $\pi(\theta)$ cannot be imputed before output vectors $X_j(\theta)$ are known, and these are not known until the investment levels I_j have been determined, but the I_js in turn cannot be chosen so as to satisfy (3.1) unless the imputed prices $\pi(\theta)$ are available. Before suggesting some possible ways out of this dilemma, a word on methodology may be in order, however.

It may be argued, not without a certain amount of justification, that the details of the process by which economic agents receive information and make production or consumption decisions is of little concern to general equilibrium theory. Appeal can be made to some loosely specified *tâtonnement* process whereby individuals and firms are led to trading positions from which no further improvements are deemed possible, and that the dynamics of this process is such that the final position in fact coincides with the equilibrium allocation as defined. In this view, the all-important fact is that to any equilibrium allocation of state contingent claims there corresponds a perfectly equivalent allocation of stocks and bonds and that there is no reason to doubt the market's ability to achieve this allocation.

It is nevertheless comforting to have at least *some* kind of description—however superficial, intuitive, or nonoperational—of a process by which a stock market equilibrium satisfying conditions (3.1) through (3.5) may be approached. Without passing judgement on their relative merits, we may consider the following two approaches.

The first approach is a kind of two-stage recontracting process where the first stage involves firms only. This stage might be conceived of as a recursive adjustment process that goes on until (3.1) and (4.6) are satisfied. For example, a set of share prices p_j may be announced, upon which firms select arbitrary investment levels I_j^0 with corresponding output vectors $X_j^0(\theta)$. The prices $\pi^0(\theta)$ that satisfy (4.6) are then computed. Using these prices, firms use (3.1) to determine new investment levels I_j^1; the corresponding $X_j^1(\theta)$ are then used to compute new imputed prices $\pi^1(\theta)$, and so on. Hopefully, this process converges. In the second stage, the output vectors resulting from the first stage (together with the share prices) are announced to individuals so that they can compute their optimal stock/bond portfolios in the manner described earlier. If demand is equal to supply for every security, equilibrium has been attained; otherwise a new set of share prices are announced and the whole process is repeated, starting with stage one. Needless to say, the process as described is not to be taken literally; all that is suggested is that the market may be thought of as behaving *as if* governed by such a process.

The second approach involves a different kind of possibility, which may exist if the production functions $\phi_j(I_j, \theta)$ have special properties that allow simplified decision rules for firms. An exhaustive list of such special cases can of course not be given; we shall illustrate here for the case of so-called *decomposable* production functions. Formally, decomposability means that the production functions can be written

$$X_j(\theta) \equiv \phi_j(I_j, \theta) = k_j(I_j) \, F_j(\theta)$$

This implies that a variation in the level of investment causes output to change by the same proportion in every state of the world, for we have here

$$\frac{dX_j(\theta)}{dI_j} \bigg/ X_j(\theta) = \frac{k_j'(I_j) \, F_j(\theta)}{X_j(\theta)}$$

$$= \frac{k_j'(I_j)}{k_j(I_j)}$$

which is independent of θ. Since

$$\phi_j'(I_j, \theta) = \frac{k_j'(I_j)}{k_j(I_j)} X_j(\theta)$$

condition (3.1) becomes

$$\frac{k_j'(I_j)}{k_j(I_j)} \sum_\theta \pi(\theta)X_j(\theta) = 1$$

or, using (4.6),

$$\frac{k_j'(I_j)}{k_j(I_j)} p_j = 1$$

In this situation, the announcement of a set of share prices p_j immediately enables firms to calculate optimal investment levels entirely without the use of imputed prices for state contingent claims.

4.5. We started our discussion of decision making in a stock market setting by stating that a prerequisite for the procedures we have described was that there be a "sufficient" number of securities available in the market. By now it should be possible to give a more precise characterization of that condition.

The condition arises, of course, from the requirement that the system of linear equations (4.6) give a unique solution for the imputed prices $\pi(\theta)$. This system consists of $n + 1$ equations (one for each security) in s unknowns (one for each state of the world). Consequently, in order to determine a unique set of imputed prices, we have to have as many linearly independent securities as there are states of the world. More formally, if R is the s-dimensional vector with all elements equal to r, then the condition is that among the $n + 1$ vectors $R, X_1(\theta), \ldots, X_n(\theta)$ there should be s vectors that are linearly independent, or, put differently, that the matrix $\{R, X_1(\theta), \ldots, X_n(\theta)\}$ is of full rank. The vector R clearly represents the output vector of the riskless industry, or the return vector of a bond. If the condition above is satisfied, we say that the stock/bond market is complete, and that we have a complete set of securities.

If the number of securities *exceeds* the number of states of the world, there would seem to be a possibility that equations (4.6) could be inconsistent. Economically, however, this would mean that the share prices were such that a pure arbitrage profit could be realized, so this situation can be ruled out. We shall discuss this in more detail in chapter 8. Note, however, that with more securities than states of the world, the determination of a stock/bond portfolio from (4.4) need not be unique for any one individual.

If there were fewer (linearly independent) securities than states of the world, infinitely many solutions to (4.6) would exist, hence no meaningful application of the optimality conditions (3.1) and (3.3) through (3.5) would be possible. Furthermore, equations (4.4) would in this case generally be inconsistent: the given securities would span only a subspace of the complete s-dimensional space, and it would generally be impossible to find a stock/bond portfolio corresponding to an arbitrary income vector $Y_i(\theta)$.

4.6. What we have shown so far is that with an incomplete set of securities we cannot, in general, be *assured* that the resulting investment levels and distributions of second-period income represents a Pareto optimum. This clearly does not mean that an incomplete stock market may *never* result in a Pareto-optimal allocation. In the chapters that follow, this is precisely the kind of possibility we shall investigate; namely, to specify conditions with respect to technology, preferences, and/or probability beliefs such that even an incomplete stock market will achieve Pareto-optimality. Now, such an investigation could clearly be justified only if we believed that incomplete security markets were empirically more relevant than complete ones. Consequently, the question arises whether or not real-world security markets can, for practical purposes, be considered complete.

At the level of abstraction on which the theory has so far been developed, there is really no meaningful way to answer that question. The reason, of course, is simply that the concept of ''state of the world'' has been rather implicitly defined. As a result, we do not have an operational method for counting the number of distinct states of the world. Although some general considerations suggest themselves, the completeness issue will probably remain as elusive as the question of how many angels can be accommodated on the point of a needle.

Consider first the concept of state of the world as a means of parametrizing randomness in production functions of firms. Suppose there are two firms which, for given investment levels, have output patterns as follows: The output of Firm 1 will be either 100 or 200 with probabilities of 1/3 and 2/3, respectively. If Firm 1's output is 100, the output of Firm 2 will be either 0 or 100 with probabilities 1/3 and 2/3, whereas if Firm 1's output is 200, Firm 2's output will be either 100 or 300 with equal probability. The situation is illustrated by the probability tree in Figure 4-1. We would in this case have to distinguish four different states of the world corresponding to each branch through the tree (in order, say, from top to bottom). The probability distribution over states of the world would then by given by $f(1) = 1/9$, $f(2) = 2/9$, $f(3) = 1/3$, $f(4) = 1/3$, and the firms' outputs as functions of the state of the world would be given as in Table 4-5.

What this example suggests, of course, is that in practice—with a large number of firms, each with a large number of possible output levels and

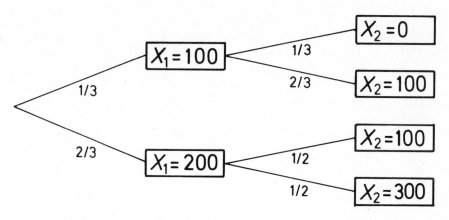

Figure 4-1. Probability Tree for Two Hypothetical Firms.

Table 4-5
Firms' Outputs as Functions of the State of the World

	State			
	1	*2*	*3*	*4*
$X_1(\theta)$	100	100	200	200
$X_2(\theta)$	0	100	100	300

with complicated stochastic dependencies among firms—the number of different states of the world needed to give a complete characterization of the uncertainty in the economy may reach astronomical proportions and exceed by far the number of securities available. And if this is the case, a stock market allocation will be Pareto-optimal only by accident.

From a less formal point of view, however, the important consideration is not really a simple comparison of the number of securities with the number of states of the world, but rather how *severe* (in terms of expected utility) is the restriction on attainable income distributions caused by an insufficient number of securities. Here again we quickly get into deep water.

First, the restriction affects different individuals differently; indeed for some individuals the restriction may not be binding at all. Second, even if individual utility losses could be calculated, there is no simple way of aggregating such losses into a meaningful measure of loss in "social welfare." Even recourse to the roughest kind of everyday intuition offers little guidance: few people seem to have any kind of feeling for what it really means to be restricted to, say, a 2000-dimensional subspace of an 80,000-dimensional space. One observation is in order, though: The suboptimality of an incomplete market gives room for an incentive to create *new* securities. The observed introduction of various kinds of hybrid securities with risk properties different from existing ones may be taken as an indication of incompleteness. The fact that existing firms frequently prefer to organize a new activity as a separate corporation rather than financing it by selling more of its own shares, suggests the same indication.

Part III
Distributive Efficiency

Introduction

The considerations in the preceding chapter suggest that the question of efficiency in a market with an incomplete set of securities is not without empirical relevance. In the literature on financial economics it seems indeed to be taken for granted that completeness of markets is a poor description of the real world.

From a methodological point of view it is possible to consider the analysis of efficiency in a complete market as a special case of a more general analysis of efficiency in financial markets. The *general* question is: Under what conditions will a competitive financial market lead to Pareto-optimality? Without making any assumptions about the number of securities as compared to the number of states of the world (and thus admitting the possibility of an incomplete set of securities), we shall see that a certain set of restrictions is required in order to ensure Pareto-optimality. In one special case however, namely, when there is a complete set of securities, the answer is different: in fact, no such restrictions need be made at all.

We noted that the complete set of allocative decisions that had to be made in the economy could be naturally subdivided into two groups. One set of decisions concerned the allocation of first-period resources among consumption C_i, investment in risky firms I_j, and riskless investment M. The other decisions concern the distribution among individuals of income available in the second period: the $Y_i(\theta)$. Corresponding to this grouping, the theoretical analysis of efficiency has also—perhaps partly by historical accident—been dichotomized.

The earliest work on Pareto-optimality of stock markets was concerned only with the distribution of output among individuals. We shall also take up this problem first, and refer to it as the problem of *distributive efficiency*.

The optimality of the allocation of first-period resources will be referred to as the *efficiency of investment*. This problem, and its relationship to the problem of distributive effciency, will be presented in Part IV.

5

Allocation of Securities versus Allocation of Income

5.1. In the analysis of distributive efficiency, we take both the consumption decisions of individuals and the investment levels of firms as exogenously given. This means that the vectors of output across states of the world are taken by individuals as given data; the trading of securities is among individuals only and does not represent any source of new investment capital for firms. Thus, we are dealing with what are usually referred to as secondary security markets, where the firms whose securities are traded play no independent roles as decision making units. The general equilibrium model of this market therefore appears as an amputated and somewhat simplified version of the model considered in chapter 4.

5.2. An individual's initial resources now have to be specified as the amount $\bar{m}_i$ of cash on hand, which is simply what he has left over after paying for his first-period consumption, and in addition the fractions $\bar{z}_{ij}$ owned of the various risky firms. His initial wealth is therefore given by

$$W_i \equiv \bar{m}_i + \sum_j \bar{z}_{ij} p_j \tag{5.1}$$

where p_j as before is the market value of the outstanding shares of company j. Both the $\bar{m}_i$ and $\bar{z}_{ij}$ are exogenously given data, and, by definition, the $\bar{z}_{ij}$ are such that

$$\sum_i \bar{z}_{ij} = 1$$

for all firms.

Using the same notation as in chapter 4 (so that m_i and z_{ij} are the individual's bond and share holdings after trading), his budget condition is written

$$m_i + \sum_j z_{ij} p_j = W_i \tag{5.2}$$

His second-period income if state of the world θ obtains is then given by

$$Y_i(\theta) = r m_i + \sum_j z_{ij} X_j(\theta)$$

which, upon substitution from the budget condition, can be written

$$Y_i(\theta) = rW_i + \sum_j z_{ij}(X_j(\theta) - rp_j) \tag{5.3}$$

Note that this formulation implies that we still take risky firms to be wholly equity financed. We shall consider the introduction of corporate debt in chapter 9.

Since the consumption decisions are left out of the model, we shall in this chapter suppress the appearance of C_i as an argument in the utility function, thus writing it simply as $u_i(Y_i)$, and hence expected utility as

$$U_i \equiv \mathcal{E}_i[u_i(Y_i)] \equiv \sum_\theta u_i(Y_i(\theta)) f_i(\theta)$$

We continue to assume that all utility functions are strictly increasing and strictly concave.

The main difference from the model of a complete stock market is that we now have to disregard the possibility of determining an optimal stock/bond portfolio indirectly as that corresponding to an optimal portfolio of state contingent claims. As we have seen, such a procedure is not generally possible, and we have therefore to express the optimality conditions directly in terms of the z_{ij}. This means that the first-order conditions for maximum expected utility are given by

$$\frac{\partial U_i}{\partial z_{ij}} = \sum_\theta u_i'(Y_i(\theta)) \frac{\partial Y_i(\theta)}{\partial z_{ij}} f_i(\theta)$$

$$= \sum_\theta u_i'(Y_i(\theta))(X_j(\theta) - rp_j) f_i(\theta)$$

$$= \mathcal{E}_i[u_i'(Y_i)(X_j - rp_j)]$$

$$= 0 \qquad (j = 1, \ldots, n) \tag{5.4}$$

where u_i' denotes the first derivative of the utility function. We have here made the standard assumption that no restrictions on short sales or margin requirements are in effect, either because there *are* no such restrictions or because the solution to (5.4) is interior relative to any such restrictions.

For each individual, the n equations (5.4) can be used to determine the z_{ij}; m_i is then determined residually from (5.2). Equations (5.4) define implicitly the individual's demands for share ownership as functions of the share prices p_j, the risk free interest rate, and parameters of the probability distribution $f_i(\theta)$. The construction of the general equilibrium model is then completed by adding the market clearing conditions

$$\sum_i z_{ij} = 1 \qquad (j = 1, \ldots, n) \tag{5.5}$$

We have then a model consisting of the m equations (5.2), the mn equations (5.4), and the n equations (5.5). To be determined are the m variables m_i, the mn variables z_{ij}, and the n company values p_j. We note that a separate market clearing condition for bonds is in this case superfluous. For by summing the budget equations over i we have

$$\sum_i m_i + \sum_i \sum_j z_{ij} p_j = \sum_i \bar{m}_i + \sum_i \sum_j \bar{z}_{ij} p_j$$

and when (5.5) is satisfied this reduces to

$$\sum_i m_i = \sum_i \bar{m}_i$$

where the right hand side is exogeneously given.

5.3. It is readily shown that the market allocation of stocks and bonds defined by the equations above represents a Pareto optimum. That is, no allocation of the given securities can be found that will make everybody at least as well off as the competitive market allocation. But this means only that as long as a central planner is restricted to effect the distribution of income by means of stocks and bonds, he can do no better (in the Pareto sense) than a competitive market. However, from a central planner's point of view it is not the allocation of stocks and bonds as such that is of primary interest, but rather the allocation of *income*. In terms of distribution of income, the stock market allocation can therefore only represent a *constrained* (or second best) Pareto optimum. Before exploring the nature of this constraint, however, let us take time out to show that no reallocation of stocks and bonds can increase some individual's expected utility without reducing that of others.

From the market clearing conditions it follows that a reallocation in the amounts dz_{ij} and dm_i must be such that

$$\sum_i dz_{ij} = 0 \qquad (j = 1, \ldots, n)$$

and

$$\sum_i dm_i = 0$$

The differentials of expected utilities are

$$dU_i = \mathcal{E}_i[u_i'(Y_i) dY_i]$$

$$= \sum_\theta u_i'(Y_i(\theta)) dY_i(\theta) f_i(\theta)$$

where

$$dY_i(\theta) = rdm_i + \sum_j X_j(\theta)dz_{ij}$$

Thus,

$$dU_i = \sum_\theta \left[u_i'(Y_i(\theta))rdm_i f_i(\theta) + u_i'(Y_i(\theta))f_i(\theta)\sum_j X_j(\theta)dz_{ij} \right]$$

$$= r\left[\sum_\theta u_i'(Y_i(\theta))f_i(\theta) \right]dm_i + \sum_j \left[\sum_\theta u_i'(Y_i(\theta))X_j(\theta)f_i(\theta) \right]dz_{ij}$$

$$= r\mathscr{E}_i[u_i'(Y_i)]dm_i + \sum_j \mathscr{E}_i[u_i'(Y_i)X_j]dz_{ij}$$

From the optimality conditions (5.4) we have that

$$\mathscr{E}_i[u_i'(Y_i)X_j] = rp_j\mathscr{E}_i[u_i'(Y_i)]$$

substitution then gives

$$dU_i = r\mathscr{E}_i[u_i'(Y_i)]dm_i + \sum_j rp_j\mathscr{E}_i[u_i'(Y_i)]dz_{ij}$$

$$= r\mathscr{E}_i[u_i'(Y_i)]\left(dm_i + \sum_j p_jdz_{ij}\right)$$

Defining $\alpha_i = 1/r\mathscr{E}_i[u_i'(Y_i)]$ this can be written

$$\alpha_i dU_i = dm_i + \sum_j p_jdz_{ij}$$

and summing over i then gives

$$\sum_i \alpha_i dU_i = \sum_i dm_i + \sum_i\sum_j p_jdz_{ij}$$

But in view of the market clearing conditions the right hand side is equal to zero, and since the α_i are positive it follows that the utility changes cannot all be of the same sign. This establishes Pareto opitmality.

5.4. As already pointed out, the optimality which we have just demonstrated is, in terms of distribution of income, a constrained one. The nature of this constraint must be clearly understood.

The most general way of describing a scheme for allocating second-period income is to determine a set of functions, one for each individual,

$$Y_i(\theta) = g_{i\theta}(rM, X_1(\theta), \ldots, X_n(\theta))$$

which specifies how much individual i is to receive if the state of the world is θ and payments from the risky firms in that state are $X_1(\theta), \ldots, X_n(\theta)$ and from riskless investment rM. Such a function is usually referred to as a *sharing rule*. There do not seem to be any a priori reasons for imposing restrictions on the functional form of these sharing rules. However, when the distribution is to be effected by stocks and bonds only, then a restriction *is* imposed on the sharing rules. From the expression (5.3) we see that such a market allows *linear* sharing rules only, whereas in a completely general arrangement the sharing rules may have any form. It is obvious that such a restriction must in general lead to a suboptimal allocation of income.

From a central planner's point of view, the only valid restrictions on the distribution of income are the feasibility constraints

$$\sum_i Y_i(\theta) = W(\theta) \qquad (\theta = 1, \ldots, s) \tag{5.6}$$

where

$$W(\theta) \equiv rM + \sum_j X_j(\theta)$$

We now wish to explore in more detail the set of Pareto-optimal sharing rules. As described in chapter 2, we can do this by maximizing a positively weighted sum of individual expected utilities subject to (5.6). The conditions for such a maximum can be derived by forming the Lagrangean

$$L = \sum_i k_i U_i + \sum_\theta \beta(\theta) \left[W(\theta) - \sum_i Y_i(\theta) \right]$$

where U_i is expected utility as defined above, and $\beta(\theta)$ the Lagrange multiplier associated with the θth of the constraints (5.6). The first-order maximum conditions are then

$$\frac{\partial L}{\partial Y_i(\theta)} = k_i u_i'(Y_i(\theta)) f_i(\theta) - \beta(\theta) = 0$$

$$(i = 1, \ldots, m; \theta = 1, \ldots, s) \tag{5.7}$$

Eliminating $\beta(\theta)$, these conditions can conveniently be written

$$k_i u_i'(Y_i(\theta)) f_i(\theta) = u_1'(Y_1(\theta)) f_1(\theta) \tag{5.8}$$

since we can arbitrarily set $k_1 = 1$. In the case of so-called *homogeneous expectations*, i.e., when the utility functions $f_i(\theta)$ are the same for all individuals, the conditions (5.8) reduce to

$$k_i u_i'(Y_i(\theta)) = u_1'(Y_1(\theta)) \tag{5.9}$$

5.5. We shall illustrate the application of the optimality conditions (5.8) with some examples.

Suppose first that all utility functions are of the simple logarithmic form $u_i(Y_i) = \ln Y_i$; equations (5.8) then become

$$\frac{k_i f_i(\theta)}{Y_i(\theta)} = \frac{f_1(\theta)}{Y_1(\theta)}$$

or

$$Y_i(\theta) = \frac{k_i f_i(\theta)}{f_1(\theta)} Y_1(\theta)$$

Summing over i and using (5.6) we then have

$$\sum_i Y_i(\theta) = \frac{\sum_i k_i f_i(\theta)}{f_1(\theta)} Y_1(\theta) = W(\theta)$$

from which we obtain the sharing rules as

$$Y_i(\theta) = \frac{k_i f_i(\theta)}{\sum_i k_i f_i(\theta)} W(\theta)$$

As a description of a particular distribution of income there is nothing problematic about such a set of sharing rules. However, if we wanted to effect them by means of stocks and bonds, problems may arise. The reason for this is that if we allow completely arbitrary probability distributions, an income vector $Y_i(\theta)$ defined by these sharing rules can be any point whatever in the s-dimensional income space, while with an incomplete set of securities only a subspace of that space is attainable. To illustrate, suppose there are two firms (no riskless income) and two individuals, and that the income vectors $X_j(\theta)$ and probability distributions $f_i(\theta)$ over three states of the world are as shown in Table 5-1. Suppose further that we have selected $k_2 = 1$; the corresponding Pareto-optimal income vectors are then seen to be as shown in Table 5-2. It is easy to verify that neither of these can be obtained as linear combinations of $X_1(\theta)$ and $X_2(\theta)$.

In the case of homogeneous expectations, however, no such problems arise. For in that case the sharing rules reduce to

$$Y_i(\theta) = \eta_i W(\theta)$$

Table 5-1
Income Vectors and Probability Distributions over Three States of the World

	State		
	1	2	3
$X_1(\theta)$	100	150	150
$X_2(\theta)$	0	100	250
$W(\theta)$	100	250	400
$f_1(\theta)$	0.1	0.3	0.6
$f_2(\theta)$	0.3	0.3	0.4

Table 5-2
Pareto-Optimal Income Vectors

	State		
	1	2	3
$Y_1(\theta)$	25	125	240
$Y_2(\theta)$	75	125	160

where

$$\eta_i \equiv \frac{k_i}{\sum_i k_i}$$

This means that each individual should receive a fixed fraction of aggregate income. Such an allocation can clearly be effected by means of stocks and bonds: it would require each individual to hold the same fraction of every outstanding security, both stocks and bonds, i.e., $m_i = \eta_i M$ and $z_{ij} = \eta_i$ for every j.

As a second illustration, consider a case where all individuals have quadratic utility functions

$$u_i(Y_i) = Y_i - c_i Y_i^2$$

Assuming homogeneous expectations, the optimality conditions become

$$k_i(1 - 2c_i Y_i(\theta)) = 1 - 2c_1 Y_1(\theta)$$

from which we get

$$Y_i(\theta) = \frac{1}{2c_i} - \frac{1}{2c_ik_i}(1 - 2c_1Y_1(\theta))$$

and hence

$$\sum_i Y_i(\theta) = \sum_i \frac{1}{2c_i} - (1 - 2c_1Y_1(\theta))\sum_i \frac{1}{2c_ik_i} = W(\theta)$$

Substituting back into the first equation, we can then solve for $Y_i(\theta)$ as

$$Y_i(\theta) = \frac{1}{2c_i} - \frac{(1/c_ik_i)}{\sum_i(1/c_ik_i)}\left(\sum_i \frac{1}{2c_i} - W(\theta)\right).$$

The noteworthy property of this relationship is that $Y_i(\theta)$ is a linear function of $W(\theta)$, i.e., it can be written in the form

$$Y_i(\theta) = a_i + b_iW(\theta)$$

where a_i and b_i are independent of $W(\theta)$. This means that also in this case a Pareto-optimal distribution of income can be effected by using stocks and bonds: the individual will have to hold bonds in the amount a_i/r and own the same fraction b_i of the shares of every risky firm.

Consider finally the income sharing between two individuals with utility functions

$$u_1(Y_1) = 2Y_1^{1/2}, \qquad u_2(Y_2) = \frac{4}{3}Y_2^{3/4}$$

Conditions (5.9) become here

$$k_2[Y_2(\theta)]^{-1/4} = [Y_1(\theta)]^{1/2}$$

Substituting $Y_2(\theta) = W(\theta) - Y_1(\theta)$ and solving for $Y_1(\theta)$, we obtain the Pareto-optimal sharing rule

$$Y_1(\theta) = [2hW(\theta) + h^2]^{1/2} - h$$

where

$$h = \frac{k_2^{-4}}{2} > 0$$

Since the sharing rule is not linear, it can in general not be effected by means of stocks and bonds—even though we have assumed homogeneous expectations.

The qualifier "in general" in the last sentence refers, of course, to the possibility of a complete set of stocks and bonds. For in that case it is always possible (for arbitrary $Y_i(\theta)$) to find an allocation of bonds m_i and shareholdings z_{ij} as a solution to the equations

$$rm_i + \sum_j z_{ij} X_j(\theta) = Y_i(\theta)$$

As noted, however, this case is not our primary concern in this chapter, and when we now discuss conditions for Pareto-optimality of a stock/bond allocation, we therefore have in mind conditions that must be satisfied in the absence of a complete set of securities (or when no completeness assumption is explicitly being made).

5.6. The three examples we went through above were meant to give an intuitive introduction to a more general analysis. The first question we want to examine is: Under what conditions is it possible to effect a Pareto-optimal distribution of income by means of stocks and bonds? We shall refer to this as the problem of *attainability*, and analyze it in the next chapter.

The next question is then: Given that the Pareto-optimal distributions of income are attainable by means of stocks and bonds, will a competitive (but incomplete) stock market in fact lead to one of the Pareto-optimal allocations? This question, which will be referred to as the question of *market optimality*, is analyzed in chapter 8. As it turns out, a prerequisite for this analysis is the establishment of certain characteristics of optimal portfolios that exhibit the so-called "separation property." A definition of this concept and the derivation of the characteristics in question are therefore interjected in chapter 7.

6 Attainability

6.1. In the following we shall derive necessary and sufficient conditions for attainability and market optimality with an incomplete set of securities. Before doing so, however, it is important to specify more precisely what we mean by necessary and sufficient conditions in this context. This is in order to set aside from the outset some possible (and frequently heard) counterexamples to the results we shall present.

The issue can conveniently be explained by defining certain sets of income allocations and illustrating relationships among these by means of set diagrams. By a set of income allocations we mean that each element of the set represents a complete specification of the sm numbers $Y_i(\theta)$ describing a distribution of second-period income among individuals across states of the world.

We thus define the following sets of income allocations:

U — the complete set of feasible income allocations.

A — the set of income allocations that are attainable by means of stocks and bonds.

P — the set of Pareto-optimal income allocations

M — the set of income allocations that can result from trading in a competitive stock market.

Clearly, both A and P are subsets of U, while M is a subset of A.

There are four groups of characteristics that together determine how the sets, A, M, and P are related to each other: (1) the utility functions $u_i(Y_i)$, (2) the probability distributions $f_i(\theta)$ and the output vectors $X_j(\theta)$, (3) the parameters k_i used to represent Pareto-optimal allocations, and (4) the initial allocations $\bar{m}_i$ and $\bar{z}_{ij}$ in a stock market. Laying down conditions for attainability or market optimality could in principle involve any of these groups of characteristics, or combinations of them. We might, for example, try to isolate those initial allocations that are sure to yield competitive stock market allocations that are Pareto-optimal. Restrictions of this kind do not seem to be of any particular theoretical or practical interest, however. The most natural approach—and the one to be followed here—is to give precedence to conditions on the utility functions; then (as needed) on the probability distributions, while imposing no restrictions at all on either the parameters k_i, the initial allocations, or the output vectors $X_j(\theta)$. The rationale for focusing on preferences and probability beliefs is clear: these are the more fundamental characteristics that even a central planner has to accept as given data.

In the absence of any restrictions on either of the characteristics listed above, the sets A, M, and P might typically be related as in Figure 6-1. In this situation, some elements of P are attainable, while others are not. When we then discuss conditions for attainability of Pareto-optimal allocations, we shall mean conditions *such that* P *is a subset of* A. With this interpretation, the observation that there exist Pareto-optimal allocations that are also attainable does not constitute a counterexample to the necessity part of the conditions. As we shall see, necessary and sufficient conditions in this sense are that all utility functions belong to a particular class of utility functions and that there are homogeneous expectations. This set of conditions is thus to be interpreted as a requirement that must be satisfied to ensure that the Pareto-optimal allocation corresponding to *any* set of values for the parameters k_i is attainable. Put differently, if this condition is not satisfied, the implication is not that it is impossible to find specific Pareto-optimal allocations that are attainable, but that an arbitrary Pareto-optimal allocation will be attainable only by accident.

Given that the conditions for attainability are satisfied, the sets of income allocations might be related as in Figure 6-2. This diagram depicts a situation where some stock market allocations are Pareto-optimal, while others are not. By conditions for market optimality we then mean conditions such that M is a subset of P. As it turns out, necessary and sufficient conditions in this sense are the same as those required for attainability. Thus, unless these conditions are satisfied we are not guaranteed that every competitive market allocation, regardless of initial allocations, is Pareto-optimal. When they are, the sets A, M, and P will be related as in Figure 6-3.

6.2. After these (somewhat lengthy) preliminaries, let us get down to the business of analyzing conditions for attainability. The Pareto-optimal sharing rules were defined by equations (5.6) and (5.7). Further, a given set of sharing rules can be effected by means of stocks and bonds if and only if they can be written in the form

$$Y_i(\theta) = \alpha_i + \sum_j \alpha_{ij} X_j(\theta) \qquad (6.1)$$

meaning that individual i is allocated bonds in the amount α_i/r and shareholdings representing the fraction α_{ij} of the shares of firm j. The question we want to answer can then be formulated as follows: Under what conditions do equations (5.6) and (5.7) have solutions for the $Y_i(\theta)$ that can be written in the form (6.1)? Although it should go without saying, we ob-

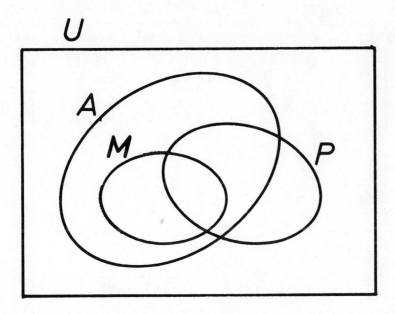

Figure 6-1. Typical Representation of Sets of Income Allocations in the Absence of Any Restrictions.

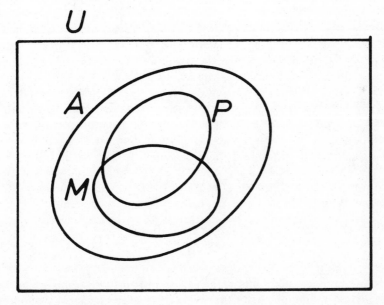

Figure 6-2. Sets of Income Allocations Given That Conditions for Attainability Are Satisfied.

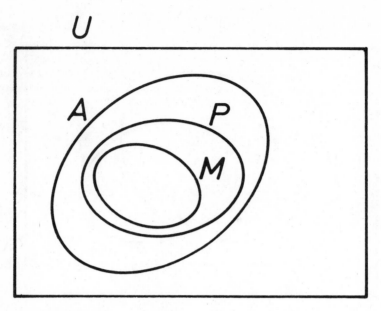

Figure 6-3. Sets of Income Allocations Given That Conditions for Market Optimality Are Satisfied.

serve for later reference that α_i and the α_{ij}, in order to represent bond and stock holdings, must be independent of θ.

We first show that whatever the conditions for attainability are, they are such that the α_{ij} in (6.1) must be the same for all j, i.e., $\alpha_{ij} = b_i$ ($j = 1, \ldots, n$). In other words, equations (5.6) and (5.7) never give solutions for $Y_i(\theta)$ in the form (6.1) unless the α_{ij} are the same for all j. The reason for this is that (5.6) and (5.7) imply that the $Y_i(\theta)$ should depend on $W(\theta)$ only—not on its individual components (or sources)—and this requirement is satisfied if and only if the α_{ij} are the same for all j.

To see why this is so, observe first that (5.7) represent conditions for a maximum of some function of the $Y_i(\theta)$ subject only to the conditions $\Sigma_i Y_i(\theta) = W(\theta)$, ($\theta = 1, \ldots, s$). This, of course, means that the optimal $Y_i(\theta)$ are functions of the $W(\theta)$, i.e., we can in general express the optimal $Y_i(\theta)$ as

$$Y_i(\theta) = F_{i\theta}(W(1), W(2), \ldots, W(s)) \qquad (6.2)$$

The fact that each $W(\theta)$ is the sum of rM and all the $X_j(\theta)$ is immaterial; these separate components of the $W(\theta)$ do not even appear in the formulation of the maximization problem. But that is not all: because of the special form of the maximand, an optimal $Y_i(\theta)$ is in fact a function of $W(\theta)$ only, so that (6.2) is of the special form

$$Y_i(\theta) = G_{i\theta}(W(\theta))$$

In other words, the optimal allocation is such that the amount to be received by an individual in any particular state depends on aggregate income in that state only, and is independent of aggregate income in any other state. To show this, we consider (5.6) and (5.7) for some particular state θ_1, and differentiate with respect to $W(\theta_2)$ where $\theta_2 \neq \theta_1$; this gives, respectively

$$\sum_i \frac{\partial Y_i(\theta_1)}{\partial W(\theta_2)} = 0 \qquad (6.3)$$

and

$$k_i u_i''(Y_i(\theta_1)) f_i(\theta_1) \frac{\partial Y_i(\theta_1)}{\partial W(\theta_2)} - \frac{\partial \beta(\theta_1)}{\partial W(\theta_2)} = 0 \qquad (6.4)$$

Here $u_i''(Y_i)$ denotes the second derivative; by the assumption of concavity of $u_i(Y_i)$, this is strictly negative. Solving (6.4) for $\partial Y_i(\theta_1)/\partial W(\theta_2)$ and summing over i gives

$$\sum_i \frac{\partial Y_i(\theta_1)}{\partial W(\theta_2)} = \frac{\partial \beta(\theta_1)}{\partial W(\theta_2)} \sum_i \frac{1}{k_i u_i''(Y_i(\theta_1)) f_i(\theta_1)}$$

which by (6.3) equals zero. But this implies that $\partial \beta(\theta_1)/\partial W(\theta_2) = 0$, and it then follows from (6.4) that we also have

$$\frac{\partial Y_i(\theta_1)}{\partial W(\theta_2)} = 0$$

which completes the proof.

We said above that given that $Y_i(\theta)$ was to be of the form (6.1) and at the same time required to depend only on $W(\theta)$, the α_{ij} would have to be the same for every j. The sufficiency of this condition is obvious, and the general necessity is also easy to see. The requirement that $Y_i(\theta)$ depend only on $W(\theta)$ implies that any zero-sum redistribution of income among firms leaves $Y_i(\theta)$ unchanged, and this will be true only when $\alpha_{ij} = b_i$ for all j. For example, any two income vectors $X_1(\theta)$ and $X_2(\theta)$ such that $X_2(\theta) = H(\theta) - X_1(\theta)$ should give the same $Y_i(\theta)$; this means that the term

$$\alpha_{i1} X_1(\theta) + \alpha_{i2}(H(\theta) - X_1(\theta))$$

should be the same for all values of $X_1(\theta)$, which in turn requires $\alpha_{i1} = \alpha_{i2}$.

A portfolio of stocks and bonds with the property that the shareholdings represent the same proportion of the outstanding shares of each risky firm will be called a *perfectly balanced* portfolio (also referred to as the *market portfolio*). Thus, in order to lead to a Pareto optimal-distribution of income, all stock/bond portfolios must be perfectly balanced. When this condition is satisfied, we see that (6.1) can be written as

$$Y_i(\theta) = \alpha_i + b_i \sum_j X_j(\theta)$$

$$= \alpha_i + b_i[W(\theta) - rM]$$

$$= (\alpha_i - b_i rM) + b_i W(\theta)$$

or, more briefly,

$$Y_i(\theta) = a_i + b_i W(\theta) \tag{6.5}$$

where $a_i \equiv \alpha_i - b_i rM$.

Again it should be emphasized that the necessity of this condition refers to a situation where no special assumptions about vectors $X_j(\theta)$ are made. There is no denying that *particular* output vectors may exist such that a Pareto-optimal allocation can be achieved with a portfolio such that the α_{ij} differ among firms. Suppose, for example, that a Pareto-optimal allocation specifies $Y_i(\theta) = \eta_i W(\theta)$ and that it so happens that $X_j(\theta) = \delta_j W(\theta)$ for all j and θ and $rM = 0$ so that $\Sigma_j \delta_j = 1$. Shareholdings α_{ij} then give

$$Y_i(\theta) = \sum_j \alpha_{ij} X_j(\theta) = W(\theta) \sum_j \alpha_{ij} \delta_j$$

so that any set of α_{ij} such that

$$\sum_j \alpha_{ij} \delta_j = \eta_i$$

satisfy the optimality conditions, and this obviously does not require all α_{ij} equal. It is equally obvious, however, that among the optimal portfolios is also the one with $\alpha_{ij} = \eta_i$ for all j. In general, a given Pareto-optimal income allocation need not imply a *unique* stock-bond allocation, but among those possible is always the one with all α_{ij} equal.

Thus, although technically speaking there are exceptions to the requirement of perfectly balanced portfolios, they really need not concern us. It remains true that a necessary condition for Pareto-optimality of a stock-bond allocation is that it can be written in the form (6.5), even though not necessarily implying perfectly balanced portfolios.

The underlying reason for nonuniqueness of a Pareto-optimal stock-bond allocation is of course the presence of stochastic dependence among the output of different firms (in the example above, they were perfectly correlated). That one security is perfectly (or highly) correlated with another or a group of others means that they are perfect substitutes and hence can be interchanged without affecting the probability distribution for portfolio return. Such nonuniqueness poses some minor technical problems in the analysis that follows, and we shall take them up as they appear.

6.3. Since any Pareto-optimal allocation of stocks and bonds gives the $Y_i(\theta)$ expressed in the form (6.5), the conditions for attainability can now be formulated as conditions under which (5.6) and (5.7) give $Y_i(\theta)$ in this form. The values for a_i and b_i will clearly depend on the values of the parameters k_i defining any particular Pareto-optimal allocation, but must, as already pointed out, be independent of θ.

We shall show that a set of necessary and sufficient conditions for attainability in this sense is that (1) *all* utility functions are such that

$$-\frac{u_i'(Y_i)}{u_i''(Y_i)} = \mu_i + \lambda Y_i \tag{6.6}$$

where the coefficients μ_i and λ are independent of Y_i; and (2) there are homogeneous expectations, i.e., $f_i(\theta) = f(\theta)$ for every i. As explained earlier, the term necessary is here to be interpreted with the qualifier "in the absence of any further restrictions on the parameters k_i."

The function $-u_i'(Y_i)/u_i''(Y_i)$ is the inverse of the Pratt-Arrow [3,1] risk aversion function, and is therefore referred to as the *risk tolerance* function (for a discussion of the significance of the risk aversion function, see the references cited above or chapter 2 in reference [2]). The first requirement is therefore that the risk tolerance functions be linear and have the *same* slope for all individuals. Apart from linear translations, the following (and only the following) forms of utility functions satisfy (6.6) (for $\mu_i \neq 0$):

Exponential: $u_i(Y_i) = -e^{-Y_i/\mu_i}$ (for $\lambda = 0$)

Logarithmic: $u_i(Y_i) = \ln(Y_i + \mu_i)$ (for $\lambda = 1$)

Power: $u_i(Y_i) = (1/\lambda - 1)(\mu_i + \lambda Y_i)^{1-1/\lambda}$ (otherwise)

Quadratic utility functions (which we used in one of our illustrations) are included in this class as the special case $\lambda = -1$. For $\mu_i = 0$, we are left with only $u_i(Y_i) = \ln Y_i$ and $u_i(Y_i) = Y_i^{1-1/\lambda}$. It should be emphasized that utility functions from the three groups cannot be "mixed": either all utility functions must be exponential, or all logarithmic, or all power functions with the same power. As we saw in the last of our illustrative examples, mixing of power functions with different powers will not give sharing rules of the linear form (6.5).

To show the necessity of (6.6), we use the optimality conditions in the form (5.8) with $Y_i(\theta)$ given by (6.5). Formally, we can consider (5.8), (5.6), and (6.5) as a system of functional equations with $u_i(Y_i)$ as the unknown functions. To find the general solution to this system, we differentiate (5.8) with respect to $W(\theta)$ and k_i, respectively; this gives

$$k_i u_i''(Y_i(\theta))b_i f_i(\theta) = u_1''(Y_1(\theta))b_1 f_1(\theta)$$

and

$$u_i'(Y_i(\theta))f_i(\theta) + k_iu_i''(Y_i(\theta))(a_{ii} + b_{ii}W(\theta))f_i(\theta)$$

$$= u_1''(Y_1(\theta))(a_{1i} + b_{1i}W(\theta))f_1(\theta)$$

Here a_{rs} (b_{rs}) denotes the derivative of a_r (b_r) with respect to k_s. Substituting from the first equation on the right hand side of the second, using the relationship $W(\theta) = (Y_i(\theta) - a_i)/b_i$ obtained from (6.5), and rearranging, we obtain

$$-\frac{u_i'(Y_i)}{u_i''(Y_i)} = \mu_i + \lambda_i Y_i \tag{6.7}$$

where μ_i and λ_i are functions of the k_i given by

$$\mu_i = k_i(a_{ii} - b_ia_{1i}/b_1) - k_ia_i(b_{ii} - b_ib_{1i}/b_1)/b_i$$

$$\lambda_i = k_i(b_{ii} - b_ib_{1i}/b_1)/b_i$$

Notice that in arriving at (6.7), the probability distributions $f_i(\theta)$ have cancelled out. Notice also that in (6.7) we have not yet restricted the λ_i to be the same for all individuals. We shall presently show that $f_i(\theta) = f(\theta)$ and $\lambda_i = \lambda$ for every i are necessary requirements in addition to (6.7).

Equation (6.7) is an elementary differential equation. The complete class of solutions for $u_i(Y_i)$ (except for linear translations) has already been given. In showing the sufficiency of (6.7) for attainability we need only the solutions in terms of marginal utility $u_i'(Y_i)$; these will have to be analyzed separately for the cases (1) $\lambda_i = 0$, and (2) $\lambda_i \neq 0$.

Case (1): $\lambda_i = 0$

The solution for u_i' is here given by

$$u_i'(Y_i) = e^{-Y_i/\mu_i}$$

and the optimality conditions (5.8) therefore become

$$k_i\exp(-Y_i(\theta)/\mu_i)f_i(\theta) = \exp(-Y_1(\theta)/\mu_1)f_1(\theta)$$

Solving for $Y_i(\theta)$ gives

$$Y_i(\theta) = \frac{Y_1(\theta)}{\mu_1}\mu_i + \mu_iA_i(\theta)$$

where

$$A_i(\theta) \equiv \ln\left(\frac{k_if_i(\theta)}{f_1(\theta)}\right)$$

In view of (5.6) we have then

$$\sum_i Y_i(\theta) = \frac{Y_1(\theta)}{\mu_1} \sum_i \mu_i + \sum_i \mu_i A_i(\theta) = W(\theta)$$

and upon substitution we obtain the sharing rules

$$Y_i(\theta) = \left[\mu_i A_i(\theta) - \frac{\mu_i}{\sum_i \mu_i} \sum_i \mu_i A_i(\theta)\right] + \frac{\mu_i}{\sum_i \mu_i} W(\theta)$$

This expression does give $Y_i(\theta)$ as a linear function of $W(\theta)$, but it is equivalent with (6.5) only if the term in brackets is independent of θ. From the definition of $A_i(\theta)$ it follows that this will be the case if and only if $f_i(\theta) = f_1(\theta)$, i.e., if there are homogeneous expectations.

Case (2): $\lambda_i \neq 0$

The solution of (6.7) is in this case given by

$$u_i'(Y_i) = (\mu_i + \lambda_i Y_i)^{-1/\lambda_i}$$

so that the optimality conditions (5.8) become

$$k_i(\mu_i + \lambda_i Y_i(\theta))^{-1/\lambda_i} f_i(\theta) = (\mu_1 + \lambda_1 Y_1(\theta))^{-1/\lambda_1} f_1(\theta)$$

Solving for $Y_i(\theta)$ gives

$$Y_i(\theta) = \frac{1}{\lambda_i}[B_i(\theta)(\mu_1 + \lambda_1 Y_1(\theta))^{-\lambda_i/\lambda_1} - \mu_i]$$

where

$$B_i(\theta) \equiv \left(\frac{f_i(\theta)}{k_i f_1(\theta)}\right)^{-\lambda_i}$$

From (5.6) we have then the condition

$$\sum_i \frac{1}{\lambda_i}[B_i(\theta)(\mu_1 + \lambda_1 Y_1(\theta))^{-\lambda_i/\lambda_1} - \mu_i] = W(\theta)$$

The form of this condition makes it apparent that it is impossible to express $Y_1(\theta)$ as a linear function of $W(\theta)$ unless $\lambda_i = \lambda_1$. We therefore conclude that a further restriction has to be imposed on the utility functions: the λ_i must be the same for all individuals, say $\lambda_i = \lambda$.

Given that $\lambda_i = \lambda$, we can solve for $Y_1(\theta)$ and then by substitution obtain the sharing rules in explicit form as

$$Y_i(\theta) = \frac{1}{\lambda}\left[\frac{B_i(\theta)}{\sum_i B_i(\theta)} \sum_i \mu_i - \mu_i\right] + \frac{B_i(\theta)}{\sum_i B_i(\theta)} W(\theta)$$

Again we have $Y_i(\theta)$ expressed as a linear function of $W(\theta)$, but not in a form that is equivalent with (6.5) unless the coefficients are independent of θ. And just as in Case (1) we see, from the definition of $B_i(\theta)$, that this will be true if and only if there are homogeneous expectations.

This completes the proof of both necessity and sufficiency of the conditions for attainability: when these are satisfied we know that it is possible to effect *any* Pareto optimum by means of some allocation of stocks and bonds. However, the fact that these are satisfied does not in itself imply that a competitive stock market allocation will be Pareto-optimal. In chapter 8 we shall show that this indeed will be true, so that whenever it is *possible* to achieve Pareto-optimality with an incomplete set of securities, the market mechanism will in fact do so. As indicated earlier, the proof of this proposition requires us to examine the so-called separation property in portfolio selection in some detail.

References

1. Arrow, K.J., "The Theory of Risk Aversion," *Essays in the Theory of Risk-Bearing*. Amsterdam: North-Holland, 1970.

2. Mossin, J., *Theory of Financial Markets,* Englewood Cliffs, N.J. Prentice-Hall, 1973.

3. Pratt, J., "Risk Aversion in the Small and in the Large," *Econometrica*, 32, 1964, pp. 122-136.

7 Separation

7.1. To define what we mean by separation, it is convenient to reformulate slightly the individual's decision problem as described in chapter 6. We therefore define the following new variables:

$$s_i \equiv \Sigma_j z_{ij} p_j$$ — total amount invested in shares by individual i.

$$x_{ij} \equiv z_{ij} p_j / s_i$$ — proportion of s_i invested in the shares of firm j (asset proportions).

$$R_j(\theta) \equiv X_j(\theta)/p_j$$ — gross return in state θ per dollar invested in firm j.

The asset proportions x_{ij} are clearly such that

$$\sum_j x_{ij} = 1$$

Earlier we expressed $Y_i(\theta)$ as in (5.3) by

$$Y_i(\theta) = rW_i + \sum_j z_{ij}(X_j(\theta) - rp_j)$$

which can be rewritten as

$$Y_i(\theta) = rW_i + s_i \sum_j \frac{z_{ij} p_j}{s_i} \left(\frac{X_j(\theta)}{p_j} - r \right)$$

In terms of the new variables we can then write $Y_i(\theta)$ as

$$Y_i(\theta) = rW_i + s_i \sum_j x_{ij}(R_j(\theta) - r)$$

or, since

$$\sum_j x_{ij} = 1$$

as

$$Y_i(\theta) = rW_i + s_i \left[\sum_j x_{ij} R_j(\theta) - r \right] \tag{7.1}$$

7.2. The concept of separation has been variously defined in the literature. We shall here consider separation as a property associated with the individual's utility function, and say that the utility function has the separation property (or allows separation) if, for arbitrary return distributions, the optimal asset proportions x_{ij} are independent of the level of wealth W_i. Note that nothing is implied about the optimal solution for s_i itself, only its relative composition.

We shall not go into the reasons for the term "separation" in connection with this property; this would carry us too far afield and is really extraneous to the purposes at hand.

By conditions for separation we mean restrictions on the utility function such that the corresponding optimal x_{ij} are the same for all values of W_i for any given but arbitrary set of return distributions $R_j(\theta)$. We shall show that a necessary and sufficient condition in this sense is that the utility function belongs to the linear risk tolerance class, i.e.,

$$-\frac{u_i'(Y_i)}{u_i''(Y_i)} = \mu_i + \lambda_i Y_i \tag{7.2}$$

It furthermore turns out that if this condition is satisfied, the optimal asset proportions vary only with λ_i (and are thus independent of μ_i).

7.3. The most well-known analysis of separation is that by Cass and Stiglitz [1]. They derive the necessity of (7.2) by establishing properties that must be satisfied by the first-order optimality conditions in order to give a solution for the x_{ij} that is independent of W_i. Although feasible, this approach appears to require rather lengthy tongue-in-cheek mathematical derivations. We shall here follow an alternative, and hopefully simpler, approach. This consists in establishing restrictions on the individual's preference ordering, from which a functional equation for the utility function is derived. This functional equation can then be reduced to the differential equation (7.2) by routine methods.

We start by defining

$$Z_i(\theta) \equiv \sum_j x_{ij} R_j(\theta) - r$$

so that (7.1) can be written as

$$Y_i(\theta) = rW_i + s_i(W_i)Z_i(\theta) \tag{7.3}$$

We have here emphasized that s_i in general may depend on W_i by using a functional notation. $Z_i(\theta)$ is clearly the amount by which return in state θ on the stock portfolio exceeds the return on riskless investment.

The choice of a particular set of asset proportions x_{ij} determines the $Z_i(\theta)$ uniquely, and $Y_i(\theta)$ depends on the x_{ij} only via $Z_i(\theta)$. By the definition of separation, the optimal x_{ij} can be chosen independently of W_i. But this must mean that the individual's preference ordering of vectors $Z_i(\theta)$ is independent of W_i, and hence that the utility function that represents this ordering is a function of Z_i only, say $v_i(Z_i)$. Suppose first that $s_i > 0$. Then the preference orderings of vectors $Y_i(\theta)$ and $Z_i(\theta)$ related to each other by (7.3) must be identical. But this implies that the utility functions $u_i(Y_i)$ and $v_i(Z_i)$ representing, respectively, these orderings are positive linear translations of each other, i.e.,

$$u_i(Y_i) = c_i v_i(Z_i) + d_i \tag{7.4}$$

with $c_i > 0$. If, on the other hand, $s_i < 0$ (the case $s_i = 0$ is obviously of no interest), then the preference orderings of vectors $Y_i(\theta)$ and $Z_i(\theta)$ must be exactly the opposite of each other. This implies that $u_i(Y_i)$ and $v_i(Z_i)$ are negative linear translations of each other, so that (7.4) holds with $c_i < 0$. In (7.4), c_i and d_i must be independent of Z_i, but they may depend on W_i. We therefore conclude that in order to allow separation, the utility function $u_i(Y_i)$ must satisfy the functional equation

$$u_i(rW_i + s_i(W_i)Z_i) = c_i(W_i)v_i(Z_i) + d_i(W_i) \tag{7.5}$$

This equation must hold as an identity in the arguments W_i and Z_i.

To find a solution to (7.5), differentiate with respect to Z_i:

$$u_i'(Y_i)s_i = c_i v_i'(Z_i) \tag{7.6}$$

Then differentiate (7.6) with respect to W_i:

$$u_i''(Y_i)(r + s_i'Z_i)s_i + u_i'(Y_i)s_i' = c_i'v_i'(Z_i) \tag{7.7}$$

Here s_i' and c_i' denote derivatives with respect to W_i. From (7.6), the right hand side of (7.7) is

$$c_i'v_i'(Z_i) = \frac{c_i's_i}{c_i} u_i'(Y_i)$$

hence (7.7) can be written

$$u_i''(Y_i)(r + s_i'Z_i)s_i + u_i'(Y_i)s_i' = \frac{c_i's_i}{c_i} u_i'(Y_i)$$

or

$$u_i''(Y_i)(r + s_i'Z_i)s_i = u_i'(Y_i)(c_i's_i/c_i - s_i')$$

so that

$$-\frac{u_i'(Y_i)}{u_i''(Y_i)} = \frac{(r + s_i'Z_i)s_i}{s_i' - c_i's_i/c_i}$$

The right hand side is a linear function of Z_i, and since Z_i is linear in Y_i, the right hand side can be written as a linear function of Y_i, i.e.,

$$-\frac{u_i'(Y_i)}{u_i''(Y_i)} = \mu_i(W_i) + \lambda_i(W_i)Y_i \qquad (7.8)$$

where the coefficients μ_i and λ_i are given by

$$\mu_i(W_i) = \frac{r(s_i - s_i'W_i)}{s_i - c_i's_i/c_i}$$

$$\lambda_i(W_i) = \frac{s_i'}{s_i - c_i's_i/c_i}$$

To complete the proof of necessity of (7.2), we have to show that the coefficients μ_i and λ_i as defined in (7.8) are constants independent of W_i. Writing for short $g_i(Y_i) \equiv -u_i'(Y_i)u_i''(Y_i)$ and differentiating (7.8) with respect to W_i and Z_i, respectively, we get

$$g_i'(Y_i)(r + s_i'Z_i) = \mu_i'(W_i) + \lambda_i'(W_i)Y_i + \lambda_i(W_i)(r + s_i'Z_i) \qquad (7.9)$$

and

$$g_i'(Y_i)s_i = \lambda_i(W_i)s_i \qquad (7.10)$$

Since these equations must hold for independent variations in Z_i and W_i it follows that both sides of (7.10) must be constant; hence λ_i is independent of W_i. But with (7.10) substituted into (7.9) and with $\lambda_i'(W_i) = 0$, it immediately follows that $\mu_i'(W_i) = 0$, which then establishes that also μ_i is independent of W_i.

Two special cases of (7.2) are worth noting: (1) If we require also s_i to be a fixed proportion of W_i, so that $s_i = s_i'W_i$ with s_i' constant, then we see that μ_i must be equal to zero. The utility function must therefore be such that $-u_i'(Y_i)/u_i''(Y_i) = \lambda_iY_i$, and we have seen in chapter 6 that the only solutions to this are

$$u_i(Y_i) = \ln Y_i \text{ (for } \lambda_i = 1)$$

and otherwise

$$u_i(Y_i) = Y_i^{1-1/\lambda}$$

(2) If we require s_i to be fixed (the same s_i for any value of W_i), so that $s_i' = 0$, then $\lambda_i = 0$ and the utility function must satisfy $-u_i'(Y_i)/u_i''(Y_i) = \mu_i$, whose only solution is

$$\mu_i(Y_i) = -e^{-Y_i/\mu_i}$$

7.4. We now turn to the sufficiency part of the condition for separation, and derive some other properties of the optimal solution when separation obtains.

In terms of the variables s_i and x_{ij}, the optimality conditions (5.4) can be written

$$\mathcal{E}_i[u_i'(Y_i)(R_j - r)] = 0 \qquad (j = 1, \ldots, n) \qquad (7.11)$$

where from (7.1) we can write $Y_i(\theta)$ as

$$Y_i(\theta) = r(W_i - s_i) + s_i \sum_j x_{ij} R_j(\theta) \qquad (7.12)$$

The n equations (7.11), together with the condition

$$\sum_j x_{ij} = 1$$

determine the $n + 1$ variables s_i and x_{ij}. We shall also here consider the optimal solution for the two cases $\lambda_i = 0$ and $\lambda_i \neq 0$ separately

Case (1): $\lambda_i = 0$

We have here

$$u_i'(Y_i) = e^{-Y_i/\mu_i}$$

or, using (7.12)

$$u_i'(Y_i(\theta)) = \exp\left\{-\frac{1}{\mu_i}\left[r(W_i - s_i) + s_i \sum_k x_{ik} R_k(\theta)\right]\right\}$$

$$= \exp\left[-\frac{1}{\mu_i} r(W_i - s_i)\right] \cdot \exp\left[-\frac{s_i}{\mu_i} \sum_k x_{ik} R_k(\theta)\right]$$

Here the first factor is nonrandom, and the conditions (7.11) therefore take the form

$$\mathcal{E}_i\left[\exp\left(-\frac{s_i}{\mu_i} \sum_k x_{ik} R_k\right)(R_j - r)\right] = 0$$

which can be written

$$\mathcal{E}_i\left[\exp\left(-h_i \sum_k x_{ik} R_k\right)(R_j - r)\right] = 0 \qquad (7.13)$$

where $h_i \equiv s_i/\mu_i$. Equations (7.13) together with the condition

$$\sum_j x_{ij} = 1$$

can be used to find a solution for h_i and the x_{ij}. Since (7.13) do not involve μ_i or W_i, the solution for h_i and the x_{ij} is independent of μ_i and W_i. We furthermore note if there are homogeneous expectations, equations (7.13) are the same for all individuals. If these equations have a unique solution, all optimal portfolios are such that

$$
\left.\begin{array}{c}
x_{ij} = x_j \\[2mm]
s_i = \mu_i h
\end{array}\right\} \qquad (i = 1, \ldots, m) \qquad \text{(7.14a)}
$$

where x_j and h is the solution of

$$
\left.\begin{array}{c}
\mathscr{E}\left[\exp\left(-h\sum_k x_k R_k\right)(R_j - r)\right] \\[3mm]
\sum_k x_k = 1
\end{array}\right\} \qquad \text{(7.14b)}
$$

If (7.14b) allow multiple solutions, different individuals may select different vectors of asset proportions, but the portfolios corresponding to different solutions will all have identical probability distributions of return and thus be equivalent from the individual's point of view. The reason for this is that since the utility function u_i is concave, expected utility

$$
U_i = \sum_\theta u_i(Y_i(\theta)) f_i(\theta)
$$

is also concave in $Y_i(1), \ldots, Y_i(s)$; therefore the vector $Y_i(\theta)$ that maximizes U_i is unique. Consequently, although different values of the x_j may satisfy the optimality conditions, the corresponding income vectors $Y_i(\theta)$ must be identical.

Case (2): $\lambda_i \neq 0$

Marginal utility is in this case

$$
u_i'(Y_i) = (\mu_i + \lambda_i Y_i)^{-1/\lambda_i}
$$

so that

$$
\begin{aligned}
u_i'(Y_i) &= \left\{\mu_i + \lambda_i\left[r(W_i - s_i) + s_i\sum_k x_{ik} R_i\right]\right\}^{-1/\lambda_i} \\[3mm]
&= \left[\mu_i + \lambda_i r(W_i - s_i) + \lambda_i s_i\sum_k x_{ik} R_k\right]^{-1/\lambda_i} \\[3mm]
&= [\mu_i + \lambda_i r(W_i - s_i)]^{-1/\lambda_i}\left[1 + \frac{\lambda_i s_i}{\mu_i + \lambda_i r(W_i - s_i)}\sum_k x_{ik} R_k\right]^{-1/\lambda_i}
\end{aligned}
$$

Since the first factor is nonrandom, the optimality conditions (7.11) become

$$\mathcal{E}_i\left\{\left[1 + h_i\sum_k x_{ik}R_k\right]^{-1/\lambda_i}(R_j - r)\right\} = 0 \qquad (7.15)$$

where

$$h_i \equiv \frac{\lambda_i s_i}{\mu_i + \lambda_i r(W_i - s_i)}$$

Again, since neither μ_i nor W_i appears in (7.15) the solution for h_i and the x_{ij} are independent of μ_i and W_i. In this case, equations (7.15) will be different for different individuals even under homogeneous expectations, unless the λ_i are the same for all individuals. If both these conditions are satisfied, however, and if in addition the solution is unique, we have

$$\left. \begin{aligned} x_{ij} &= x_j \\[2ex] s_i &= \frac{h(\mu_i + \lambda r W_i)}{\lambda(1 + hr)} \end{aligned} \right\} \qquad (i = 1, \ldots, m) \qquad (7.16a)$$

where h and the x_j are determined by

$$\left. \begin{aligned} \mathcal{E}&\left\{\left[1 + h\sum_k x_k R_k\right]^{-1/\lambda}(R_j - r)\right\} = 0 \\[2ex] &\sum_k x_k = 1 \end{aligned} \right\} \qquad (7.16b)$$

If (7.16b) has multiple solutions, exactly the same comments apply as in case (1).

References

1. Cass, D., and J.E. Stiglitz, "The Structure of Investor Preferences and Asset Returns, and Separability in Portfolio Allocation: A Contribution to the Pure Theory of Mutual Funds," *Journal of Economic Theory*, 2, 1970, pp. 122-160.

8 Market Optimality

8.1. We can now return to the analysis of the conditions under which a competitive stock market (for any set of initial allocations) will lead to a Pareto-optimal distribution of income. As indicated at the end of chapter 6, these conditions are in fact the same as those required for attainability, namely, that all utility functions belong to the linear risk tolerance class with the same λ for all individuals, and homogeneous expectations. We shall proceed by showing that under these conditions, and only then, will the following two propositions be true:

(1) Each market determined portfolio has a return distribution which is identical with that of a perfectly balanced portfolio so that the $Y_i(\theta)$ are of the form (6.5):

$$Y_i(\theta) = a_i + b_i W(\theta);$$

(2) The a_i and b_i corresponding to the market allocation satisfy conditions (5.8) for Pareto-optimality.

The formulation under (1) is clearly related to the discussion in chapter 6 where we pointed out that (6.5), because of the possibility of linear dependence among the $X_j(\theta)$, need not necessarily require perfectly balanced portfolios.

8.2. In the preceding chapter we showed that individuals would choose portfolios either such that $x_{ij} = x_j$ for all i, or such that the probability distributions for portfolio return are identical with such portfolios, if and only if all utility functions belong to the linear risk tolerance class (with the same λ for all individuals) and there were homogeneous expectations. As before, the necessity of these conditions is to be interpreted as requirements that must be satisfied for arbitrary combinations of W_i, λ_i, and $f_i(\theta)$. Note that this property refers to individual optimal portfolios for given, but arbitrary, security prices. We now show that in market equilibrium portfolios are perfectly balanced if and only if optimal asset proportions are the same for all individuals. But it is clear that it makes no difference whether portfolios in fact have the same asset proportions and hence in equilibrium are perfectly balanced as long as the corresponding probability distributions for portfolio return are identical with those for portfolios with these properties.

Suppose first that $x_{ij} = x_j$ for all individuals, i.e., from the definition of x_{ij},

$$\frac{z_{ij}p_j}{\sum\limits_k z_{ik}p_k} = x_j \qquad (i = 1, \ldots, m)$$

Solving for z_{ij} we get

$$z_{ij} = \frac{x_j}{p_j}\sum_k z_{ik}p_k \qquad (8.1)$$

and summation over i gives

$$\sum_i z_{ij} = \frac{x_j}{p_j}\sum_i\sum_k z_{ik}p_k$$

$$= \frac{x_j}{p_j}\sum_k p_k\sum_i z_{ik}$$

so in view of the market clearing conditions (5.5) we have

$$\frac{x_j}{p_j}\sum_k p_k = 1$$

or

$$\frac{x_j}{p_j} = \frac{1}{\sum\limits_k p_k}$$

Substituting back in (8.1) then gives

$$z_{ij} = \frac{\sum\limits_k z_{ik}p_k}{\sum\limits_k p_k}$$

But the right hand side is the same for every j, hence $z_{ij} = z_i$ for every j.

Conversely, if $z_{ij} = z_i$, it follows from the definition of the asset proportions that

$$x_{ij} = \frac{z_{ij}p_j}{\sum z_{ik}p_k}$$

$$= \frac{z_i p_j}{\sum z_i p_k}$$

$$= \frac{p_j}{\sum p_k}$$

which is the same for all individuals. This establishes both necessity and sufficiency of the given conditions for perfectly balanced portfolios. This means that (5.3) can be written

$$Y_i(\theta) = rW_i + z_i \sum_j (X_j(\theta) - rp_j)$$

$$= r\left(W_i - z_i \sum_j p_j\right) + z_i(W(\theta) - rM)$$

$$= r\left[W_i - z_i\left(\sum_j p_j + M\right)\right] + z_i W(\theta)$$

or

$$Y_i(\theta) = a_i + b_i W(\theta) \tag{8.2}$$

where

$$a_i = r\left[W_i + z_i\left(\sum_j p_j + M\right)\right]$$

and $b_i = z_i$.

This completes the proof of our first proposition. The intuitive explanation for this result is quite simple. Assume there are two firms in the economy with total share values of $p_1 = 100$ and $p_2 = 200$, and suppose that at these prices all individuals wish to divide their share investment with 40% in the first firm and 60% in the second: $x_{i1} = 0.4$, $x_{i2} = 0.6$ for all i. Of course, this is just not possible, since the value of the first firm constitutes only one third of the total. Share prices simply cannot be equilibrium prices unless they generate optimal asset proportions which equal the fractional part of the security's market value, i.e.,

$$x_{ij} = \frac{p_j}{\sum_k p_k}$$

8.3. We now proceed to the second proposition: that the market determined values of a_i and b_i as defined above satisfy the conditions for Pareto-optimality. We consider the two solution forms for $u_i'(Y_i)$ separately.

Case (1)

With $Y_i(\theta) = a_i + b_i W(\theta)$ we have in this case

$$u_i'(Y_i(\theta)) = \exp\left[-\frac{1}{\mu_i}(a_i + b_i W(\theta))\right]$$

and

$$u_1'(Y_1(\theta)) = \exp\left[-\frac{1}{\mu_1}(a_1 + b_1 W(\theta))\right]$$

Taking logarithms and eliminating $W(\theta)$ between these two expressions, we can solve for $u_1'(Y_1(\theta))$ in terms of $u_i'(Y_i(\theta))$ as

$$u_1'(Y_1(\theta)) = C_i[u_i'(Y_i(\theta))]^{D_i} \qquad (8.3)$$

where

$$C_i \equiv \exp\left(\frac{a_i b_1}{\mu_1 b_i} - \frac{a_1}{\mu_1}\right)$$

$$D_i \equiv \frac{\mu_i b_1}{\mu_1 b_i}$$

With homogeneous expectations, the conditions for Pareto-optimality are given by (5.9), and it is clear that (8.3) satisfies this condition if—and only if—the power D_i as defined above equals unity, i.e., if

$$\frac{b_i}{\mu_i} = \frac{b_1}{\mu_1}$$

Thus, the market allocation is Pareto-optimal if and only if

$$\frac{z_i}{\mu_i} = \frac{z_1}{\mu_1} \qquad (i = 1, \ldots, m)$$

But for this class of utility functions we had from (7.14) that

$$s_i \equiv \sum_j z_{ij} p_j = z_i \sum_j p_j = \mu_i h$$

hence

$$\frac{z_i}{\mu_i} = \frac{h}{\sum_k p_j}$$

Since the right hand side is the same for all individuals, the proposition follows.

Case (2)

Here,

$$u_i'(Y_i(\theta)) = [\mu_i + \lambda(a_i + b_i W(\theta))]^{-1/\lambda}$$

and similarly for $u_1'(Y_1(\theta))$. By eliminating $W(\theta)$, we can express $u_1'(Y_1(\theta))$ in terms of $u_i'(Y_i(\theta))$ as

$$u_1'(Y_1(\theta)) = \left\{ \mu_1 + \lambda a_1 - \frac{b_1}{b_i}(\mu_i + \lambda a_i) + \frac{b_1}{b_i}[u_i'(Y_i(\theta))]^{-\lambda} \right\}^{-1/\lambda}$$

which satisfies (5.9) if and only if

$$\mu_1 + \lambda a_1 - \frac{b_1}{b_i}(\mu_i + \lambda a_i) = 0$$

i.e.,

$$\frac{\mu_i + \lambda a_i}{b_i} = \frac{\mu_1 + \lambda a_1}{b_1} \qquad (i = 1, \ldots, m)$$

From (8.2) we had a_i given by $a_i = r[W_i - z_i(\Sigma p_j + M)]$, hence the market allocation is Pareto-optimal if and only if the expression

$$G_i \equiv \frac{\mu_i + \lambda r \left[W_i - z_i \left(\sum_j p_j + M \right) \right]}{z_i} \tag{8.4}$$

is the same for all individuals. But for this class of utility functions we had from (7.16) that

$$s_i = z_i \sum_j p_j = \frac{h(\mu_i + \lambda r W_i)}{\lambda(1 + hr)}$$

so that

$$z_i = \frac{h(\mu_i + \lambda r W_i)}{\lambda(1 + hr) \sum_j p_j}$$

Substituting this in (8.4), G_i reduces to

$$G_i = \frac{\lambda}{h} \sum_j p_j - rM$$

which is the same for all i, and the proposition follows.

8.4. This completes the formal analysis of Pareto-optimality of an incomplete stock market. Because the securities available in such a market restrict the set of attainable distributions of income, seemingly strong restrictions—on both utility functions and probability distributions—have to be satisfied in order to ensure market optimality.

From a practical point of view, the significance of these restrictions is again less then clearcut. There is clearly no use denying that the real world may include individuals whose choice behavior is inconsistent with a utility function of the linear risk tolerance class, or who disagree with others about the likelihood of certain states of the world occuring. The question, rather is whether the conditions for market optimality can reasonably be accepted as approximations and therefore admitted as working hypotheses for practical purposes. Such an assumption might be justified along different lines.

First, behavior consistent with utility functions of the linear risk tolerance class does not seem unreasonable. An important member of this class is the logarithmic, which has a number of properties to recommend itself as a candidate for "everyman's utility function" (see reference [1]). Particularly from a long run point of view, portfolio selection policies that do not maximize the expectation of a logarithmic utility function may lead to very undesirable consequences.

Alternatively, we may appeal to the well-known mean-variance approach to portfolio selection. This, of course, is the approach almost universally adopted (and thus implicitly recommended) in textbooks on portfolio selection and has among practitioners come to be virtually synonymous with portfolio selection. Now, any portfolio that is mean-variance efficient in the sense of this approach also maximizes the expectation of some quadratic utility function and these, as we noted, are members of the linear risk tolerance class. Thus, if we accept portfolio selection according to some mean-variance criterion as generally descriptive of individual behavior, we are in the clear.

A related, but basically different, argument runs in terms of characteristics of the probability distribution for portfolio return. There is evidence both theoretical (central limit theorem) and empirical that return distributions for well-diversified portfolios may be closely approximated by two-parameter distributions. In that case any optimal portfolio would be mean-variance efficient. Further, we would expect any reasonable set of preferences to induce a fairly well-diversified portfolio. Therefore, regardless of the individual's preferences, he will select a portfolio that is, for all practical purposes, efficient. This in turn means that the conditions for market optimality may be satisfied.

Finally, as far as homogeneity of expectations is concerned, it may be argued (see chapter 5 in reference [2]) that this assumption, at least as an approximation, may not really be such a terribly unrealistic assumption after all. Particularly when the number of individuals is large it seems intuitively reasonable to expect that individual deviations from some average of individuals' probability estimates will be of minor importance for the attainment of a Pareto-optimal distribution of income.

Some further speculations, involving "near-completeness" of actual security markets, were offered towards the end of chapter 4, and need not be repeated here.

8.5. In chapter 4 we saw that when there are as many linearly independent securities as there are states of the world, then a competitive stock market allocation will be Pareto-optimal for arbitrary utility functions and probability distributions. It will be recalled that the argument we gave for this proposition involved an (imaginary) shadow market for state contingent claims, and proceeded as follows: with a complete set of securities the individual can infer a set of prices $\pi(\theta)$ for state contingent claims by solving equations (4.6):

$$\left.\begin{aligned} \sum_\theta \pi(\theta)X_j(\theta) &= p_j \\ \sum_\theta \pi(\theta) &= 1/r \end{aligned}\right\}$$

Next, using these prices, the individual can determine an optimal portfolio $Y_i(\theta)$ of state contingent claims by maximizing $\sum_\theta u_i(Y_i(\theta))f_i(\theta)$ subject to the budget condition

$$\sum_\theta \pi(\theta)Y_i(\theta) = W_i$$

Finally, when the $Y_i(\theta)$ have been so determined, he can determine the corresponding portfolio of the original securities . (i.e., m_i and the z_{ij}), this time by solving the equations (4.4)

$$rm_i + \sum_j z_{ij}X_j(\theta) = Y_i(\theta)$$

Then, since we know that a market allocation of state contingent claims is Pareto-optimal it follows that the corresponding (and, as far as distribution of income is concerned, identical) stock market allocation also is Pareto-optimal.

Many will find that this roundabout argument is not only cumbersome, but presupposes a considerable degree of sophistication in individual decision making. For this reason it may be instructive to conclude this chapter with a more direct demonstration of the distributive efficiency of a complete stock market, i.e., without going via a shadow market for state contingent claims.

Assume first that there are exactly as many securities as there are states of the world, i.e., $n + 1 = s$ (or $n = s - 1$), and that they are all linearly independent. The market allocation satisfies the demand equations for shares (5.4):

$$\mathcal{E}_i[u_i'(Y_i)(X_j - rp_j)] = 0$$

which can be written in full as

$$\sum_\theta u_i'(Y_i(\theta))(X_j(\theta) - rp_j)f_i(\theta) = 0 \qquad (j = 1, \ldots, n) \qquad (8.5)$$

Define

$$\xi_i(\theta) \equiv u_i'(Y_i(\theta))f_i(\theta)$$

and

$$A_j(\theta) \equiv X_j(\theta) - rp_j$$

Then (8.5) becomes

$$\sum_\theta A_j(\theta)\xi_i(\theta) = 0 \qquad (j = 1, \ldots, n) \qquad (8.6)$$

For each individual, this represents a system of $s - 1$ equations in s variables $\xi_i(\theta)$. By the assumption of linear independence, the matrix $A_j(\theta)$ will be of full rank. Consequently, we have one degree of freedom in determining the $\xi_i(\theta)$. Suppose that for individual 1 we have given a value for $\xi_1(1)$; then the remaining $\xi_1(\theta)$ ($\theta = 2, \ldots, s$) are uniquely determined as the solution to

$$\sum_{\theta=2}^{s} A_j(\theta)\xi_1(\theta) = -A_j(1)\xi_1(1)$$

Now, if for individual i ($i \neq 1$), the value of $\xi_i(1)$ constitutes the multiple γ_i of $\xi_1(1)$, i.e., $\xi_i(1) = \gamma_i\xi_1(1)$, then the remaining $\xi_i(\theta)$ ($\theta = 2, \ldots, s$) are determined by

$$\sum_{\theta=2}^{s} A_j(\theta)\xi_i(\theta) = -A_j(1)\gamma_i\xi_1(1)$$

But by multiplying the right hand side of every equation in a system of linear equation by the same factor γ_i we change the solution by that factor; this means that we must have

$$\xi_i(\theta) = \gamma_i\xi_1(\theta)$$

for *every* θ. Therefore, the only solutions admitted by (8.6) for different individuals are such that $\xi_i(\theta) = \gamma_i\xi_1(\theta)$ for every i and θ. But from the definition of $\xi_i(\theta)$ this implies

$$u_i'(Y_i(\theta))f_i(\theta) = \gamma_i u_1'(Y_1(\theta))f_1(\theta)$$

which are the conditions (5.8) for Pareto-optimality. In other words, when we have as many linearly independent securities as states of the world, the fact that the market allocation satisfies (5.4) implies that the optimality conditions (5.8) also are satisfied.

If, on the other hand, there are fewer linearly independent securities than states of the world, then the rank of the matrix $A_j(\theta)$ is less than $s - 1$, so that equations (8.6) allow solutions for different individuals that are not proportional; hence we have no guarantee of Pareto-optimality.

If there were more securities than states of the world, the system (8.6) would contain at least as many equations as unknowns. However, the maximum rank of $A_j(\theta)$ must still equal $s - 1$, so that the results above follow. To illustrate, suppose $s = 3$ and that the vectors $X_1(\theta)$, $X_2(\theta)$, and R with all elements equal to r, are linearly independent. If we now add an extra security $X_3(\theta)$, it must necessarily be possible to express it as a linear combination of the others, say,

$$X_3(\theta) = \delta_1 X_1(\theta) + \delta_2 X_2(\theta) + \delta_3 R$$

But then the market value of $X_3(\theta)$, p_3, must necessarily be such that

$$p_3 = \delta_1 p_1 + \delta_2 p_2 + \delta_3$$

since otherwise a pure arbitrage profit could be realized. Consequently,

$$X_3(\theta) - rp_3 = \delta_1(X_1(\theta) - rp_1) + \delta_2(X_2(\theta) - rp_2)$$

or

$$A_3(\theta) = \delta_1 A_1(\theta) + \delta_2 A_2(\theta)$$

Hence the rank of $A_j(\theta)$ is only two. Quite generally, the rank of $A_j(\theta)$ is one less than the number of linearly independent securities.

References

1. Hakansson, N.H., "Capital Growth and the Mean-Variance Approach to Portfolio Selection," *Journal of Financial and Quantitative Analysis*, 1971, pp. 77-91.

2. Mossin, J., *Theory of Financial Markets*, Englewood Cliffs, N.J. Prentice-Hall, 1973.

9

Capital Structure Theory

9.1. At least superficially, this chapter could be considered a digression from the main topic of the book. There is, however, a very intimate relationship between capital structure theory and the theory of capital market efficiency. It would not be unreasonable, indeed, to expect that a security market that can effect an efficient distribution of income is also a market where purely financial reorganizations will make no difference.

The capital structure problem as a theoretical issue goes back, of course, to 1958 with the publication of Modigliani and Miller's article [1]. Their propositions seemed to reject most of the conventional wisdom in the area of corporate finance: the value of the firm was independent of its capital structure and its method of financing irrelevant in evaluating an investment project. What these propositions amounted to was nothing less than the assertion that, under the assumed conditions, financial problems just didn't exist.

Such conclusions were naturally met with incredulity among financial practitioners and scepticism among their academic counterparts. The search went out for an explanation, and since the logic of their argument seemed to hold water, that explanation would have to be found in the assumptions underlying their theory. Little did they know at the time that this direction of pursuit represented a sidetracking from the real issue.

Nevertheless, the literature during the last decade has to some extent succeeded in clarifying a number of misconceptions surrounding the Modigliani-Miller propositions. To begin with, the chief villain of the plot was thought to be the so-called "risk class assumption." It now seems clear that this "assumption" is of no particular relevance and may actually have tended to confuse our understanding of the propositions. It also seemed unclear whether the presence of default risk on the firm's debt played a role in the argument; we now know that default risk in itself *need* not invalidate the propositions, although in the absence of default risk, they will always be true. Also, the *ceteris paribus* nature of these propositions has become more widely recognized.

What nobody denies, however, is the importance of tax provisions and other forms of market "imperfections," for corporate financing decisions. It is, in fact, not unusual to find the practical teaching of finance based on models whose sole source of empirical content are such imperfections. While for many purposes such an approach may be quite appro-

Table 9-1
Two-Firm Economy

	State of the world		Market Values
	1	2	
$X_1(\theta)$	100	150	120
$X_2(\theta)$	0	100	40
$W(\theta)$	100	250	—

priate and useful, we shall here continue to be concerned with a world without taxes or other imperfections and undertake, as it were, a re-examination of the Modigliani-Miller theory. "A Re-examination of the Modigliani-Miller Theorem" is in fact the title of Stiglitz's important paper [2], and our discussion owes much to his penetrating analysis.

9.2. To bring out some of the ideas involved, we shall start by considering a simple illustrative example. Thus, suppose we have an economy with two firms with second-period income $X_1(\theta)$ and $X_2(\theta)$ in two states of the world, and market values p_1, p_2 as given in Table 9-1. $W(\theta)$ denotes total income $X_1(\theta) + X_2(\theta)$. We assume that both firms are wholly equity financed, and that shareholdings in the two firms are the only investment opportunities available.

Consider now an individual who has a total investment capital of 40 available. If we denote his holdings in the two companies by z_1 and z_2, his investment budget is given by

$$120z_1 + 40z_2 = 40$$

With holdings z_1 and z_2 his income in state θ is given by

$$Y(\theta) = X_1(\theta)z_1 + X_2(\theta)z_2$$

Substituting $z_2 = 1 - 3z_1$ from the budget equation we can write

$$Y(\theta) = X_2(\theta) + [X_1(\theta) - 3X_2(\theta)]z_1$$

i.e.,

$$Y(1) = 100z_1$$

$$Y(2) = 100 - 150z_1$$

Eliminating z_1 between these expressions, we obtain the individual's *opportunity set* for income in the two states of the world represented by

$$Y(2) = 100 - \frac{3}{2}Y(1)$$

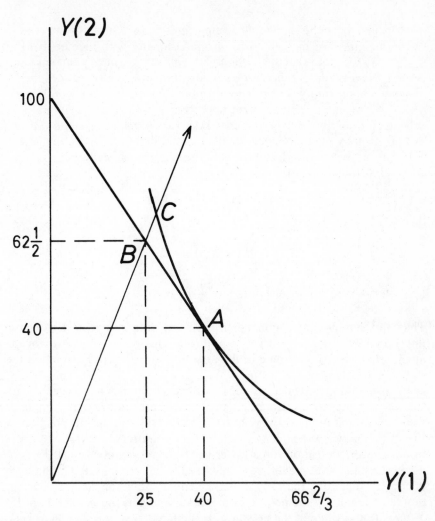

Figure 9-1. Opportunity Sets for an Individual in the Two-Firm Economy.

In Figure 9-1, this set of feasible income combinations is given by the straight line intersecting the axes at $Y(2) = 100$, $Y(1) = 66\frac{2}{3}$. For example, if the individual so chooses, he may obtain the perfectly riskless portfolio $Y(1) = Y(2) = 40$ (the point labelled A) by holding a 40% interest in Company 1 and taking a short position for 20% of the stock of Company 2 ($z_1 = 0.4$, $z_2 = -0.2$).[a]

---

[a] An indifference curve in the $Y(1)$, $Y(2)$ plane is the locus of points such that $f(1)u(Y(1)) + f(2)u(Y(2)) = $ const. If the utility function is concave (implying risk aversion) such indifference curves are convex.

Consider now the individual's opportunities in a situation where the two companies are merged to form one company with income $W(\theta) = X_1(\theta) + X_2(\theta)$. Note that such a merger represents a purely financial operation. Nevertheless, this reorganization quite drastically reduces the individual's opportunity set for income in the two states of the world: since there is now only one investment opportunity available, the only attainable income combination is such that $Y(1)/Y(2) = 0.4$. Denote the value of the new firm by p and the individual's interest in it by z. Assuming as before that his initial wealth is 40, z must necessarily be such that $z = 40/p$ and therefore his income such that

$$Y(\theta) = X(\theta)z = 40X(\theta)/p$$

that is,

$$Y(1) = \frac{4{,}000}{p}$$

$$Y(2) = \frac{10{,}000}{p}$$

Thus, in Figure 9-1, his income distribution must lie somewhere along the line $Y(2) = 2.5Y(1)$, the precise point depending upon p. Suppose, for example, that the market value of the new firm turns out to be equal to the sum of the values of the old firms, i.e., $p = p_1 + p_2 = 160$. Then his income distribution will be $Y(1) = 25$, $Y(2) = 62.5$ (point B in Figure 9-1). As we see, this point was also attainable when shares in the two companies were sold separately. However, if the individual's preferred position in that situation was the point A (or any other point different from B), he is now in a worse position (on a lower utility level) than before. If he is to attain the same utility level, he would have to be compensated in the form of a lower value of p than 160 so that he could obtain the income distribution represented by the point C. For example, if C is the point $Y(1) = 28$, $Y(2) = 70$, the value of the new firm would have to be $p = 142.86$ to keep the individual undamaged. Only if his preferred position in the original situation was such that he held the same proportion of both companies ($z_1 = z_2 = 0.25$, corresponding to the point B) would he be indifferent to a situation where $p = p_1 + p_2$. A portfolio containing the same proportion of all available securities is what we earlier referred to as a *perfectly balanced* portfolio.

The purpose of this example has been to cast doubt upon the validity of what is referred to as the "additivity property" of market values, i.e., on the proposition that the market value of a sum of income streams is equal to the sum of the market values of the separate income streams. When two income streams are combined into one, the effect is in general to reduce possibilities for diversification and hence to narrow down individuals' opportunity sets. Intuitively, we would expect this to make investment in shares less attractive relative to first-period consumption, and thus lead to lower share prices. As a result, we would not expect the additivity property to hold.

The underlying reason for this has been indicated at several points before. In the example, we moved from a situation with a complete set of securities to one with only an incomplete set, thus shrinking the set of attainable distributions of income. This will, except under special circumstances, lead to a less preferred position for some or all individuals. This will be true of any financial reorganization that reduces the dimensionality of the subspace of attainable distributions of income.

9.3. The reader may by now have started to wonder what all this has to do with Modigliani and Miller's capital structure propositions. This will be apparent if we give the following alternative interpretaion of the variables in our example: there is only one company in the economy with income $W(\theta)$. In what we called the first situation, the company has outstanding debt promising to pay 150. In state 1 the company will default on this obligation so that bondholders receive 100 while shareholders receive nothing. In state 2 the bondholders receive their due of 150, while the shareholders receive the remaining 100. Thus, $X_1(\theta)$ represents the return on bonds and $X_2(\theta)$ the return on shares. Then, what we called the second situation is one where the company has no debt. Thus, what we have been trying to get across is that there is no reason to expect the total value of the firm to be the same in the two situations—contrary to the Modigliani-Miller proposition. We shall now examine this proposition more closely.

The Modigliani-Miller argument is carried out in terms of a comparison of the market values of two firms that have identical vectors of second-period income, thus differing only in their capital structure. Specifically, we shall take Company 1 to be wholly equity financed, while Company 2, in addition to its shares, has issued a certain amount of bonds which, by definition, represent a preferred claim on the firm's income. We illustrate by means of a numerical example involving three states of the world, as given in Table 9-2.

We here use the following notation for company j:

$X_j(\theta)$ — total second-period income.

$B_j(\theta)$ — second-period income claimed by bondholders.

$R_j(\theta)$ — second-period income claimed by shareholders.

v_j — total market value of the firm.

b_j — market value of bonds.

p_j — market value of shares.

Table 9-2
Two-Firm Economy with Identical Vectors of Second-Period Income

	State of the world			Market Values
	1	*2*	*3*	
$R_1(\theta) = X_1(\theta)$	100	250	400	$v_1 = p_1$
$B_2(\theta)$	100	150	150	b_2
$R_2(\theta)$	0	100	250	p_2
$B_2(\theta) + R_2(\theta) = X_2(\theta)$	100	250	400	$v_2 = b_2 + p_2$

By definition, $B_j(\theta) + R_j(\theta) = X_j(\theta)$ and $v_j = b_j + p_j$. Since the distribution of total income (i.e., its "operating risk") is the same for both firms, we have $X_1(\theta) = X_2(\theta) = X(\theta)$ for all θ. Since Company 1 has no debt, $R_1(\theta) = X_1(\theta)$ and $v_1 = p_1$. We assume, however, that the bonds of Company 2 promise to pay 150; as we see, this obligation will be defaulted on if state 1 should occur.

In this situation, there are altogether three securities available in the market. Consider now an individual holding some (arbitrary) portfolio consisting of a fraction α of the shares of Company 1, a fraction β of the bonds of Company 2, and a fraction γ of the shares of Company 2. The cost of such a portfolio is

$$\alpha v_1 + \beta b_2 + \gamma p_2$$

and it will give the income distribution

$$Y(\theta) = \alpha X_1(\theta) + \beta B_2(\theta) + \gamma R_2(\theta)$$

Since $X_1(\theta) = X_2(\theta) = B_2(\theta) + R_2(\theta)$, $Y(\theta)$ can alternatively be written

$$Y(\theta) = \alpha[B_2(\theta) + R_2(\theta)] + \beta B_2(\theta) + \gamma R_2(\theta)$$

$$= (\alpha + \beta)B_2(\theta) + (\alpha + \gamma)R_2(\theta)$$

Thus, precisely the same income distribution can be obtained by holding the fraction $\alpha + \beta$ of the bonds, and the fraction $\alpha + \gamma$ of the shares, of Company 2. The cost of this portfolio is

$$(\alpha + \beta)b_2 + (\alpha + \gamma)p_2 = \alpha(b_2 + p_2) + \beta b_2 + \gamma p_2$$

$$= \alpha v_2 + \beta b_2 + \gamma p_2$$

Since the two portfolios give identical income distributions they must cost the same; otherwise a pure arbitrage profit could be realized. Thus, we must have

$$\alpha v_1 + \beta b_2 + \gamma p_2 = \alpha v_2 + \beta b_2 + \gamma p_2$$

implying $v_1 = v_2$.

Because of the linear dependence among the three securities $[X_1(\theta) = B_2(\theta) + R_2(\theta)]$, there are obviously many more ways of constructing portfolios that give the same income distribution; there are, in fact, infinitely many such portfolios. For any of these, the requirement that their cost be the same would imply that $v_1 = v_2$.

From the observation that the total values of the two firms must be the same, the Modigliani-Miller proposition would seem to follow without further ado. After all, since Company 1 has *no* debt and Company 2 *has* debt, must not company value be independent of the level of debt? Such a conclusion does not follow from the premise, however: *the fact that* $v_1 = v_2$ *does not imply this (common) value is the same for different levels of Company 2's debt. What is more, this will in fact be the exception rather than the rule.* We shall try to explain why this is so in the context of our illustrative example.

With only two linearly independent securities, the set of attainable income distributions constitutes a plane, i.e., a subspace, in the three-dimensional income space. This plane can be generated by combinations of any two of the three securities; for concreteness we shall consider portfolios consisting of the bonds and shares of Company 2. Thus with the assumed debt level of 150, the attainable income distributions are those representing linear combinations of the vectors

$$B_2^1(\theta) = \begin{Bmatrix} 100 \\ 150 \\ 150 \end{Bmatrix}, \qquad R_2^1(\theta) = \begin{Bmatrix} 0 \\ 100 \\ 250 \end{Bmatrix}$$

In Figure 9-2, this opportunity set may be represented by a plane such as that through the points a_1, b_1. Consider now what happens if the company has an alternative debt level, say one that promises to pay 300. This promise will be defaulted on in both states 1 and 2, so that the payments to bondholders and shareholders, respectively, are given by the vectors

$$B_2^2(\theta) = \begin{Bmatrix} 100 \\ 250 \\ 300 \end{Bmatrix}, \qquad R_2^2(\theta) = \begin{Bmatrix} 0 \\ 0 \\ 100 \end{Bmatrix}$$

and the set of attainable income distributions are those representing linear combinations of these two vectors. It is obvious that this opportunity set is different from the opportunity set generated by the vectors $B_2^1(\theta)$ and $R_2^1(\theta)$. For example, the income distribution

$$Y(\theta) = \begin{Bmatrix} 40 \\ 70 \\ 85 \end{Bmatrix}$$

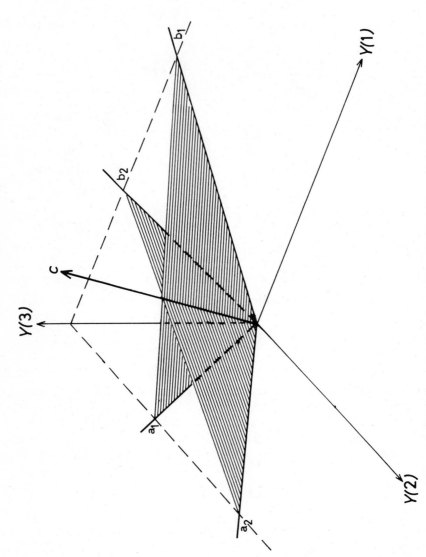

Figure 9-2. Opportunity Sets in a Three-Dimensional Income Space.

is attainable with the vectors $B_2^1(\theta)$ and $R_2^1(\theta)$ $\quad[Y(\theta) = 0.4B_2^1(\theta) + 0.1R_2^1(\theta)]$, but not attainable by a combination of $B_2^2(\theta)$ and $R_2^2(\theta)$. On the other hand is the income distribution

$$Y(\theta) = \begin{Bmatrix} 20 \\ 50 \\ 70 \end{Bmatrix}$$

attainable with the vectors $B_2^2(\theta)$ and $R_2^2(\theta)$ $\quad[Y(\theta) = 0.2B_2^2(\theta) + 0.5R_2^2(\theta)]$, but not with the vectors $B_2^1(\theta)$ and $R_2^1(\theta)$.

In Figure 9-2 the opportunity set generated by $B_2^2(\theta)$ and $R_2^2(\theta)$ is some plane such as that through the points a_2, b_2. From the figure it is apparent that there are income distributions attainable under *either* debt level, namely, those lying along the line from the origin through the point c, and representing the intersection of the two planes. This ray is evidently the locus of income distributions obtained from perfectly balanced portfolios, i.e., income distributions of the form $Y(\theta) = \gamma X(\theta)$. To see why, consider an arbitrary portfolio consisting of the fractions β and γ of respectively, the bonds and shares of Company 2; the return on this portfolio is thus

$$Y(\theta) = \beta B_2(\theta) = \gamma R_2(\theta)$$

Substituting $R_2(\theta) = X_2(\theta) - B_2(\theta)$, this can be written

$$Y(\theta) = (\beta - \gamma)B_2(\theta) + \gamma X_2(\theta)$$

If the vector $Y(\theta)$ is to be the same for any vector $B_2(\theta)$ (i.e., independent of the debt level), we must clearly have $\beta = \gamma$. A change in the company's debt level therefore corresponds to a rotation of the opportunity plane around the axis $\gamma X(\theta)$, and only for an individual whose portfolio is perfectly balanced will alternative debt levels be a matter of indifference.

We now see why the Modigliani-Miller proposition does not generally hold. As long as there are fewer (linearly independent) securities than there are states of the world, the set of attainable income distributions is restricted to a subspace in the income space. When debt levels are changed (or other financial reorganizations undertaken), the set of attainable income distributions also changes. But when the set of attainable income distributions changes, the equilibrium prices also change, and generally in such manner that the total value of the securities issued by a given firm changes.

9.4. We should now also be able to see more clearly the conditions under which company values are, in fact, independent of capital structure. The first and most obvious case is when we have a complete set of securities, since then any distribution of income is attainable anyhow, and individuals' opportunity sets thus remain unchanged under financial reorganizations.

A second case where (even in the absence of a complete set of securities) changes in a firm's debt level are of no consequence is when these changes are in the range where there is no probability of default, i.e., for debt levels below $\min_\theta X_j(\theta)$. To see this, suppose the firm has a debt level that will pay the amount d in every state of the world, thus giving share owners $X_j(\theta) - d$; consider further an individual whose portfolio includes a fraction α of the company's bonds and a fraction β of the company's shares. His income from these holdings is thus

$$Y(\theta) = \alpha d + \beta(X_j(\theta) - d) \tag{9.1}$$

Suppose now that the firm's debt level instead had been d' [but also less than $\min_\theta X_j(\theta)$]. The individual could then obtain exactly the same distribution of income by continuing to hold the fraction β of the company's shares but changing his holding of its bonds to

$$\alpha' = \frac{d}{d'}\alpha + \frac{d' - d}{d'}\beta$$

For with these holdings, his income would be

$$Y'(\theta) = \alpha' d' + \beta(X_j(\theta) - d')$$

$$= \left[\frac{d}{d'}\alpha + \frac{d' - d}{d'}\beta\right]d' + \beta(X_j(\theta) - d')$$

$$= \alpha d + \beta(X_j(\theta) - d)$$

which is identical with (9.1). Consequently, the set of attainable income distributions is invariant with respect to the debt level.

Let b_j and p_j be the market values of the firm's bonds and shares, respectively, when the debt level is d, and b_j' and p_j' when the debt level is d'. The cost to the individual of the portfolios described above are then

$$\alpha b_j + \beta p_j$$

and

$$\left[\frac{d}{d'}\alpha + \frac{d' - d}{d'}\beta\right]b_j' + \beta p_j'$$

in the two situations. Since they give identical distributions of income they must necessarily cost the same, i.e., we must have

$$\alpha b_j + \beta_j p_j = \left[\frac{d}{d'}\alpha + \frac{d' - d}{d'}\beta\right]b_j' + \beta p_j'$$

or

$$\left[b_j - \frac{d}{d'} b_j'\right]\alpha + \left[p_j - \frac{d' - d}{d'} b_j' - p_j'\right]\beta = 0$$

This equality must hold for any set of values for α and β; this requires both expressions in brackets to be zero. Solving for b_j' and p_j' gives

$$b_j' = \frac{d'}{d} b_j$$

$$p_j' = p_j - \frac{d' - d}{d} b_j$$

and consequently

$$b_j' + p_j' = p_j + b_j$$

Thus, the total market value of the firm is the same under either debt level.

The conditions of either a complete set of securities or of riskless bonds are both such that individuals' opportunity sets remain unchanged under alternative financial arrangements. If neither of these conditions are satisfied, we have seen that there remains only one set of circumstances under which individuals are indifferent to financial arrangements, namely, when their equilibrium portfolios are perfectly balanced. This condition is of a nature entirely different from the other two. When this condition is satisfied, individuals' preferred income distributions all lie in a very special subset of the income space, namely, that subset which is the intersection of the subspaces of attainable income distributions generated under all possible financial arrangements. Thus, all individuals can obtain their preferred income distributions under any set of financial arrangements; hence the equilibrium values of firms are unaffected by their capital structures.

By now the intimate relationship between the question of the role of capital structure and the question of distributive efficiency of capital markets should be clear: the conditions under which capital structure is irrelevant and the conditions under which a market allocation of securities gives a Pareto-optimal distribution of income are in fact the same. With a complete set of securities either characteristic follows; with incomplete markets the conditions is for both propositions that equilibrium portfolios be perfectly balanced. The corresponding requirements in terms of preferences and probability beliefs were spelled out in detail in chapter 8. Thus, not only is a market effecting distributive efficiency also one where financial arrangements make no difference: the converse also holds true.

The practical difference between alternative financial arrangements is, after all, only that of channeling given income streams different ways.

What we have now established is that in (and only in) an efficient market does company value depend on the total income stream and not on how it is channeled to the market.

References

1. Modigliani, F., and M.H. Miller, "The Cost of Capital, Corporation Finance, and the Theory of Investment," *American Economic Review*, 1958, pp. 261-297.

2. Stiglitz, J.E., "A Re-examination of the Modigliani-Miller Theorem," *American Economic Review*, 1969, pp. 784-793.

**Part IV
Efficiency of Investment**

Introduction

We now turn to face the problems connected with the determination and Pareto-optimality of the first-period investment decisions of firms and (less prominently) the consumption decisions of individuals. In chapter 3, these decisions were analyzed under the assumption of complete markets. Our concern here, then, is with the restrictions imposed by an incomplete set of securities. We shall see that this raises problems with respect to an appropriate formulation of company objectives and our conception of the firm as a price taker. This has to do with the fact that the lack of a complete set of securities introduces certain kinds of monopolistic elements in the market.

The literature we shall review has a number of important features in common. First, all problems concerned with distributive efficiency are "assumed away," either by explicitly restricting attention to constrained Pareto optima, i.e., such as could be effected by means of stocks and bonds, or by making assumptions about preferences and expectations such that an incomplete stock market actually achieves distributive efficiency. Second—and in view of our discussion in the preceding chapter, this follows more or less as a corollary—the Modigliani-Miller capital structure proposition is assumed to hold, so that the method of financing the firm's investments is immaterial. As a consequence, we shall in what follows for the most part assume that firms are wholly equity financed.

Finally, it is assumed that some form of company ownership has been established prior to the current trading and investment.

10 Share Price Maximization

10.1 The traditional starting point for the analysis of the firm's investment decisions has been the premise that in order to serve the interests of its shareholders the firm should evaluate alternative levels of investment in terms of their effect on the *price per share*. According to this criterion an investment is considered acceptable if its effect is to raise the price per share, and an optimal level of investment would be one that maximizes the price per share. As we shall see later, the correspondence between this objective and shareholders interests need not be as obvious as it may appear. However, we shall take share price maximization as a useful point of departure, and explore its implications as we go along.

10.2 Consider now a firm that has currently n_j shares outstanding, has a debt level d_j, a total market value of v_j, and hence a market value of equity of $p_j = v_j - d_j$ and a price per share of p_j/n_j. Suppose the firm considers an investment project which costs an amount I to undertake, and which has been estimated will increase the firm's market value to $v_j' = v_j + \Delta v_j$. (How this estimate has been made is for the moment immaterial.) It is instructive to consider the effect of such an investment on the price per share in the case of both debt and equity financing.

With debt financing the new debt level becomes

$$d_j' = d_j + I$$

so that the new market value of equity will be calculated as

$$p_j' \equiv v_j' - d_j'$$
$$= v_j + \Delta v_j - d_j - I$$
$$= p_j + \Delta v_j - I$$

and thus the new price per share as

$$\frac{p_j'}{n_j} = \frac{p_j + \Delta v_j - I}{n_j}$$

since the number of shares outstanding is the same as before. The change in the price per share is therefore

$$\frac{p_j' - p_j}{n_j} = \frac{\Delta v_j - I}{n_j} \tag{10.1}$$

99

With financing through a public offering of shares, the number of outstanding shares is increased to n_j'; the new issue thus consists of $n_j' - n_j$ shares, and the issue required to finance the investment must then satisfy

$$\frac{p_j'}{n_j'}(n_j' - n_j) = I$$

where p_j'/n_j' is the new price per share. Solving for n_j' gives

$$n_j' = \frac{p_j' n_j}{p_j' - I}$$

so that the new price per share is such that

$$\frac{p_j'}{n_j'} = \frac{p_j' - I}{n_j}$$

The new value of equity is in this case calculated as

$$p_j' = v_j + \Delta v_j - d_j$$
$$= p_j + \Delta v_j$$

and hence the new price per share is

$$\frac{p_j'}{n_j'} = \frac{p_j + \Delta v_j - I}{n_j}$$

The increase in the price per share is then

$$\frac{p_j'}{n_j'} - \frac{p_j}{n_j} = \frac{\Delta v_j - I}{n_j}$$

which is identical with (10.1).

To complete the picture we also consider the case of a rights issue, where existing shareholders are offered new shares at a price below market price on a privileged-subscription basis. If the offering price is a, the new issue must consist of I/a shares, so that $n_j' = n_j + I/a$. With $p_j' = p_j + \Delta v_j$, the new price per share *ex rights* becomes

$$\frac{p_j'}{n_j'} = \frac{p_j + \Delta v_j}{n_j + I/a}$$

so that the value of the right to buy one new share is

$$\frac{p_j'}{n_j'} - a = \frac{p_j + \Delta v_j}{n_j + I/a} - a$$

The number of old shares required to buy one new share is

$$\frac{n_j}{n_j' - n_j} = \frac{an_j}{I}$$

so that the rights price (per old share) is

$$\left(\frac{p_j + \Delta v_j}{n_j + I/a} - a\right)\frac{I}{an_j}$$

For existing shareholders the relevant effect is that on the price per share *rights on*, which is then given by

$$\frac{p_j + \Delta v_j}{n_j + I/a} + \left(\frac{p_j + \Delta v_j}{n_j + I/a} - a\right)\frac{I}{an_j} = \frac{p_j + \Delta v_j - I}{n_j}$$

regardless of the offering price a. This represents an increase from the original price of $(\Delta v_j - I)/n_j$, which is also identical with (10.1).

That the effect is the same under either method of financing clearly follows from the assumption that company value is independent of capital structure. Thus, quite generally, the requirement that the investment be such that it raises the price per share (rights on, if any) translates into the condition that $\Delta v_j \geq I$, which simply says that the increase in company value should exceed the cost of the investment.

As an example, consider a company that initially has a share value of 750 and a debt level of 250 and thus a total value of 1000. The company has the opportunity to make an investment which it estimates will increase its total value by 250; according to the criterion above this will be acceptable as long as its cost is less than 250. Suppose the cost is 200 and that the number of shares initially outstanding is 100, each with a price of 7.50. From (6.1) we can calculate that the price per share will rise by 0.50 to 8.00. With debt financing, this is seen to agree with the fact that in this case the new value of equity would be calculated as $1250 - 450 = 800$, or a price per share of 8.00. A public issue would at this price require 25 new shares in order to bring in the capital needed, thus increasing the number of shares outstanding to 125. With unchanged debt level the new value of equity will be 1000, which is consistent with a price of 8.00 per share. Consider finally a rights offering at a price of 4.00 per share. This requires a new issue of 50 shares, implying $n_j' = 150$ and a new price ex rights of $1000/150 = 6.67$. The value of the right to buy one new share is thus $6.67 - 4.00 = 2.67$. Old shareholders can in this case buy one new share for every two old shares, and the rights price is therefore 1.33, giving a price per share rights on of $6.67 + 1.33 = 8.00$. Whether an old shareholder exercises his right or not is immaterial. A shareholder originally owning two shares (worth 15.00) will, if he exercises his right, after an outlay of 4.00 be the owner of three shares worth 6.67 each; this represents a gain of

1.00. If instead he sells his rights for 1.33 each, he will have 2.67 in cash plus his two shares now worth 13.33, which also represents a gain of 1.00.

10.3 Having thus demonstrated the irrelevance of the method of financing the firm's investment, we shall for the rest of the book take firms to be wholly equity financed and any new financing to be effected by a public share offering. This means that from now on p_j represents both the total value of the firm and the value of its equity.

In the following we shall consider the level of investment I as a continuous variable and the market value of the firm as a concave, differentiable function of I. In that case investment is profitable as long as $dp_j/dI \geq 1$ and (assuming this condition to be satisfied for some I) the investment level that maximizes the price per share is such that $dp_j/dI = 1$. I.e., investment is pushed to the point where the increase in company value caused by the last dollar of investment is just equal to that investment.

11 Diamond's Model

11.1. The seminal paper on Pareto-optimality of investment in a complete stock market is that by Diamond [1]. His characterization of the stock market is very much the same as that presented in chapter 4, except that (in our terms) he takes the first-period consumption decisions by individuals as exogeneously given. Thus, we define

$$s_i \equiv q_i - C_i$$

as individual i's exogeneously given stock of investment capital, and correspondingly, for the economy as a whole,

$$S \equiv \sum_i s_i \equiv Q - \sum_i C_i$$

as the given supply of investment capital. The first-period feasibility constraint then becomes

$$\sum_j I_j + M = S$$

Otherwise the notation is as before.

11.2. Individual i owns—in addition to his stock of investment capital—initially $\bar{n}_{ij} = \bar{z}_{ij}\bar{n}_j$ shares in company j, so that his initial wealth is defined by

$$W_i = s_i + \sum_j \bar{n}_{ij}\frac{p_j}{n_j}$$

where n_j is generally different from $\bar{n}_j$ as a result of the firm's share issue (cf. equation (4.2)). His budget condition is then

$$m_i + \sum_j z_{ij}p_j = W_i$$

where $z_{ij} = n_{ij}/n_j$ (cf. equation (4.3)), and his second-period income correspondingly

$$Y_i(\theta) = rm_i + \sum_j z_{ij}X_j(\theta)$$

103

which, after substitution from the budget equation, can be written

$$Y_i(\theta) = rW_i + \sum_j z_{ij}(X_j(\theta) - rp_j)$$

(cf. equation (5.3)). Finally, his demand equations for shares are given by the first-order conditions for maximum expected utility as

$$\mathscr{E}_i[u_i'(Y_i)(X_j - rp_j)] = 0 \qquad (j = 1, \ldots, n) \tag{11.1}$$

(cf. equation (5.4)).

11.3. Turning to the behavior of firms, Diamond makes two important assumptions. The first is essentially of a technological nature, namely, that all production functions are of the decomposable type that we briefly introduced towards the end of chapter 4. That is, it is assumed that the production functions are of the form

$$X_j(\theta) \equiv \phi_j(I_j, \theta) = k_j(I_j) F_j(\theta)$$

As pointed out earlier, this formulation implies that a variation in the level of investment causes output to change by the same proportion in every state of the world:

$$\frac{dX_j(\theta)}{dI_j} \bigg/ X_j(\theta) = \frac{k_j'(I_j)}{k_j(I_j)}$$

This means that a change in the level of investment represents a pure scale-changing operation (or a so-called nondiversifying investment). Note that this assumption does not necessarily imply constant returns to scale in the firm's operations: a increase in I_j by one percent may well increase output in every state of the world by more or less than one percent.

The second assumption is more in the nature of a behavioral assumption and essentially represents a particular specification of the firm as a price taker. We shall refer to it as the *proportionality assumption*; it says that with a production function such that output will change by the same percentage in every state of the world, the firm will base its investment decision on the belief that the value of the firm will change by that same percentage. Thus it is assumed that the relationship between company value p_j and its level of investment is such that

$$\frac{dp_j}{dI_j} \bigg/ p_j = \frac{dX_j(\theta)}{dI_j} \bigg/ X_j(\theta)$$

so that

$$\frac{dp_j}{dI_j} = \frac{k_j'(I_j)}{k_j(I_j)} p_j \tag{11.2}$$

If the firm—given the proportionality assumption—seeks to maximize the price per share, it will then select an investment level satisfying

$$\frac{k_j'(I_j)}{k_j(I_j)} p_j = 1 \qquad (11.3)$$

In Diamond's paper, the proportionality assumption was apparently accepted as a matter of course. However, it is not as innocuous as it perhaps may seem. Its meaning is most clearly seen in terms of a perceived schedule of market demand for the firm's shares. Note first that integration of (11.2) implies that the firm uses a valuation formula of the explicit form

$$p_j = c_j k_j(I_j) \qquad (11.4)$$

where c_j is a constant independent of I_j. Consider now a schedule relating market demand for the firm's shares to the price per share. For such a schedule to have any meaning, the probability distribution for return per share must be the same at different values for the number of shares outstanding. With the given production function, this is achieved only by having the number of shares equal (or proportional) to $k_j(I_j)$ so that

$$\frac{X_j(\theta)}{n_j} = \frac{X_j(\theta)}{k_j(I_j)} = F_j(\theta)$$

In that case, (11.4) implies that the price per share is given by

$$\frac{p_j}{n_j} = c_j$$

independently of I_j (or n_j). Therefore, the proportionality assumption is equivalent to the assumption that the firm believes that it faces a perfectly elastic demand schedule for its shares; in other words that it can sell unlimited numbers of shares with identical probability distributions for return per share at a fixed price.

The reason why the firm's optimal level of investment has to be characterized in the implicit form (11.3) is clearly that although the firm believes that p_j is proportional to $k_j(I_j)$, it does not know what the factor of proportionality is. The optimality condition could of course also have been obtained by differentiation of (11.4) as

$$\frac{dp_j}{dI_j} = c_j k_j'(I_j) = 1$$

but since it is only known that $c_j = p_j/k_j(I_j)$, this condition must be expressed in the form (11.3).

We shall explore the proportionality assumption in more detail later; suffice it here only to say that as a valuation model it is open to objections and is not generally valid.

11.4. The general equilibrium model is now completed by adding the market clearing conditions for shares given, as before, by

$$\sum_i z_{ij} = 1 \qquad (j = 1, \ldots, n) \tag{11.5}$$

so that

$$\sum_i n_{ij} = n_j$$

The optimality conditions (11.3) are then most naturally considered as the firm's demand functions for investment capital which in turn define their supply schedules for shares. That is, if a "market manager" announces a set of share prices p_j, firms can use (11.3) to calculate optimal investment levels I_j and from that determine the corresponding share issue by the condition

$$\frac{p_j}{n_j}(n_j - \bar{n}_j) = I_j$$

Given these investment levels, the output distributions $X_j(\theta)$ are determined, and individuals can use (11.1) to calculate their optimal z_{ij} and quote the corresponding number of shares they are prepared to hold: $n_{ij} = z_{ij}n_j$. If then $\Sigma_i n_{ij} = n_j$ the trade is effected; otherwise recontracting starts. By a trivial repetition of the proof given at the beginning of chapter 4, we find that at market equilibrium the feasibility constraints on first-period use of resources and second-period distribution of output will be satisfied, i.e., we have

$$\sum_i m_i + \sum_j I_j = S \tag{11.6a}$$

$$\sum_i Y_i(\theta) = rM + \sum_j X_j(\theta) \qquad (\theta = 1, \ldots, s) \tag{11.6b}$$

We note that the demand (supply) schedules (11.3) make sense only if the production functions exhibit (stochastically) decreasing returns to scale, i.e., are such that $k_j'' < 0$. For the second-order condition for a maximum is that

$$\frac{d^2 p_j}{dI_j^2} = \frac{k_j''(I_j)}{k_j(I_j)} p_j < 0$$

which clearly requires $k_j'' < 0$. Under increasing returns to scale the derivative (11.2) is clearly everywhere positive, implying that no finite optimal value of I_j exists. Increasing returns to scale would mean that we were faced with exactly the same inconsistency as that encountered in classical market theory between increasing returns and perfect competition; acting as price takers, firms with increasing returns to scale would expand output to the extent that they would influence prices, and thus not be price takers after all.

11.5. We now proceed to show that when investment levels that staisfy (11.3) are chosen, the resulting market allocation represents a Pareto optimum. As usual, we do this by showing that no reallocation in the neighborhood of the market allocation can increase everybody's expected utility. We therefore consider a reallocation $\{dI_j, dm_i, dz_{ij}\}$ which in view of (11.5) and (11.6a) must satisfy

$$\sum_i dm_i + \sum_j dI_j = 0$$

$$\sum_i dz_{ij} = 0 \qquad (j = 1, \ldots, n)$$

The changes in $X_j(\theta)$ are given by

$$dX_j(\theta) = k_j'(I_j) \, F_j(\theta) dI_j$$

$$= \frac{k_j'(I_j)}{k_j(I_j)} X_j(\theta) dI_j$$

In equilibrium (11.3) holds, hence

$$dX_j(\theta) = \frac{X_j(\theta)}{p_j} dI_j$$

The changes in $Y_i(\theta)$ are then given by

$$dY_i(\theta) = rdm_i + \sum_j X_j(\theta)dz_{ij} + \sum_j z_{ij}dX_j(\theta)$$

$$= rdm_j + \sum_j X_j(\theta)dz_{ij} + \sum_j z_{ij}\frac{X_j(\theta)}{p_j} dI_j$$

so that the changes in expected utilities become

$$dU_i = \mathcal{E}_i[u_i'(Y_i)dY_i]$$

$$= \mathcal{E}_i\left[u_i'(Y_i)\left(rdm_i + \sum_j X_jdz_{ij} + \sum_j z_{ij}\frac{X_j}{p_j} dI_j\right)\right]$$

$$= r\mathscr{E}_i[u_i'(Y_i)]dm_i$$

$$+ \sum_j \mathscr{E}_i[u_i'(Y_i)X_j]dz_{ij}$$

$$+ \sum_j \frac{z_{ij}}{p_j} \mathscr{E}_i[u_i'(Y_i)X_j]dI_j$$

From (11.1) we have

$$\mathscr{E}_i[u_i'(Y_i)X_j] = rp_j\mathscr{E}_i[u_i'(Y_i)]$$

hence

$$dU_i = r\mathscr{E}_i[u_i'(Y_i)]dm_i + r\mathscr{E}_i[u_i'(Y_i)]\sum_j p_j dz_{ij}$$

$$+ r\mathscr{E}_i[u_i'(Y_i)]\sum_j z_{ij}\,dI_j$$

Letting $\alpha_i \equiv 1/r\mathscr{E}_i[u_i'(Y_i)]$ this can be written

$$\alpha_i dU_i = dm_i + \sum_j p_j dz_{ij} + \sum_j z_{ij}dI_j$$

and thus

$$\sum_i \alpha_i dU_i = \sum_i dm_i + \sum_i \sum_j p_j dz_{ij} + \sum_i \sum_j z_{ij}dI_j$$

$$= \sum_i dm_i + \sum_j p_j \sum_i dz_{ij} + \sum_j dI_j \sum_i z_{ij}$$

Here

$$\sum_i dz_{ij} = 0$$

and

$$\sum_i z_{ij} = 1$$

but we are then left with

$$\sum_i dm_i + \sum_j dI_j$$

which also equals zero, hence

$$\sum_i \alpha_i dU_i = 0$$

and the proposition follows. To reiterate: with the given technology and behavior according to the proportionality assumption, the resulting stock market allocation of investment capital among firms is efficient.

This result is by no means without interest, but the special nature of the underlying model should be kept in mind.

First, the assumed investment behavior of firms (and portfolio selection by individuals) imply only a *constrained* Pareto optimum in the sense defined earlier, i.e., *given* that second-period income is to be distributed by means of stocks and bonds, no reallocation can increase everybody's expected utility.

Second, the case of decomposable production functions is a very special one and hence of limited interest from a practical point of view. It may in particular be noted that a model formulation in terms of such production functions excludes from consideration stochastic dependence among outputs of different firms. What is more, we shall see that these production functions cannot be generalized without at the same time altering the specification of the firm's decision making behavior.

Finally, as already noted, the proportionality assumption is open to objections. For one thing, it is clearly inseparably connected with the assumption of decomposable production functions; indeed, without decomposable production functions the proportionality assumption is just meaningless. More important, however, is the fact that even as a valuation model for proportional output changes, the proportionality assumption is generally not valid. When equilibrium has been attained, firms will observe that the basis on which they have made their investment decisions is in fact wrong. This clearly reduces the attractiveness of (11.3) as part of a general equilibrium model.

11.6. When the decomposability assumption is dropped it remains true, of course, that a company will want to carry investment to the point where $dp_j/dI_j = 1$ in order to maximize price per share. However, for this more general case Diamond had no simple valuation model on which firms could be assumed to base their calculations, and was therefore unable to come up with a rule for competitive investment whose efficiency properties could be examined. There seem to be several reasons for this. First, he did not make full use of the general equilibrium conditions, since market clearing conditions are not invoked in the analysis. Second, he made no specific assumptions about individuals' preferences. Third, he allowed individuals to have heterogeneous expectations. At the loss of a certain amount of generality in these respects, the so-called Sharpe-Lintner-Mossin (SLM) mean-variance general equilibrium model does allow us to derive an explicit market valuation formula that can be used to calculate equilibrium values for firms with completely arbitrary output patterns. This model was the basis for subsequent work on investment optimality, particularly papers by Stiglitz [4], Jensen and Long [2], and Merton and Subrahmanyam [3]. An added bonus from this approach is that it allows explicit consideration of stochastic dependence among different firms' outputs. Before exploring these developments, however, we shall have to give a presentation of the mean-variance valuation model itself.

References

1. Diamond, P., "The Role of a Stock Market in a General Equilibrium Model with Technological Uncertainty," *American Economic Review*, 1967, pp. 759-776.

2. Jensen, M., and J. Long, "Corporate Investment under Uncertainty and Pareto Optimality in the Capital Markets," *Bell Journal of Economics and Management Science*, 1972, pp. 151-174.

3. Merton, R.C., and M.G. Subrahmanyam, "The Optimality of a Competitive Stock Market," *Bell Journal of Economics and Management Science*, 1974, pp. 145-170.

4. Stiglitz, J.E., "On the Optimality of the Stock Market Allocation of Investment," *Quarterly Journal of Economics*, 1972, pp, 25-60.

12   Mean-Variance Valuation

12.1. As suggested in the preceding chapter, the SLM model is a general equilibrium model which, on the basis of specific assumptions about individual preferences and probability assessments, generates an explicit expression for the market value of firms with arbitrary production functions (or distributions of output). These assumptions are (1) that each individual selects a portfolio that is *mean-variance efficient*, and (2) that there are homogeneous expectations in the market.

That a portfolio is mean-variance efficient means that among feasible portfolios with the same mean it has the smallest possible variance and that, at the same time, it has the largest mean among those with the same variance. This concept is typically illustrated geometrically as in Figure 12-1, where the shaded area represents the set of feasible mean-variance combinations while the curve defining its southeast boundary between A and B represents the the locus of efficient mean-variance combinations. Note that the term "efficient" in this context has a meaning entirely different from elsewhere in this book, where it is synonymous with "Pareto-optimal."

12.2. With portfolio return (second-period income) for individual i given by

$$Y_i(\theta) = rW_i + \sum_j z_{ij}(X_j(\theta) - rp_j)$$

the mean E_i and variance V_i can be expressed in terms of the expected values of outputs $\mu_j \equiv \mathscr{E}[X_j(\theta)]$ and the covariances between outputs $\sigma_{jk} \equiv \mathscr{E}(X_j(\theta) - \mu_j)(X_k(\theta) - \mu_k)]$ (σ_{jj} is then the variance of firm j's output). Thus,

$$E_i \equiv \mathscr{E}[Y_i(\theta)] = rW_i + \sum_j z_{ij}(\mu_j - rp_j)$$

and

$$V_i \equiv \mathscr{E}[Y_i(\theta) - E_i]^2$$

$$= \mathscr{E}\left[\sum_j z_{ij}(X_j(\theta) - \mu_j)\right]^2$$

111

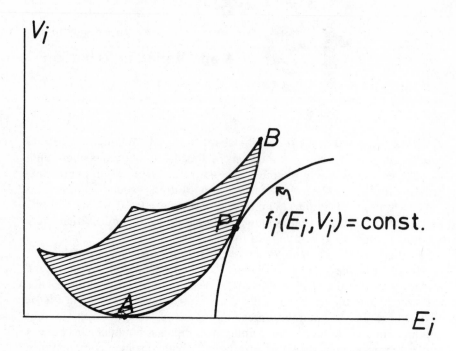

Figure 12-1. Representation of Mean-Variance Efficiency.

$$= \mathscr{E}\left\{\left[\sum_j z_{ij}(X_j(\theta) - \mu_j)\right]\left[\sum_k z_{ik}(X_k(\theta) - \mu_k)\right]\right\}$$

$$= \mathscr{E}\left[\sum_j \sum_k z_{ij}z_{ik}(X_j(\theta) - \mu_j)(X_k(\theta) - \mu_k)\right]$$

$$= \sum_j \sum_k z_{ij}z_{ik}\mathscr{E}[(X_j(\theta) - \mu_j)(X_k(\theta) - \mu_k)]$$

$$= \sum_j \sum_k z_{ij}z_{ik}\sigma_{jk}$$

A mean variance efficient portfolio can now be characterized as a portfolio that maximizes some preference function of the form

$$U_i = f_i(E_i, V_i) \tag{12.1}$$

with

$$\frac{\partial U_i}{\partial E_i} \equiv f_{iE} > 0$$

$$\frac{\partial U_i}{\partial V_i} \equiv f_{iV} < 0$$

Geometrically, such a function can be thought of as generating indifference curves in the E_i, V_i-plane, and the efficiency locus then appears as the locus of points of tangency between an indifference curve and the set of feasible mean-variance combinations. Because of the assumption of homogeneous expectations, all individuals will perceive the efficiency locus as the same, but different individuals may select different points along this curve, reflecting differences in attitude to risk. A point near A represents the portfolio of an individual with strong risk aversion, while the opposite is true of points near B.

The first-order conditions for a maximum of (12.1) are given by

$$\frac{\partial U_i}{\partial z_{ij}} = f_{iE}\frac{\partial E_i}{\partial z_{ij}} + f_{iV}\frac{\partial V_i}{\partial z_{ij}}$$

$$= f_{iE}(\mu_j - rp_j) + 2f_{iV}\sum_k z_{ik}\sigma_{jk}$$

$$= 0$$

or

$$\sum_k z_{ik}\sigma_{jk} = \beta_i(\mu_j - rp_j) \qquad (j = 1, \ldots, n) \qquad (12.2)$$

where

$$\beta_i \equiv -\frac{f_{iE}}{2f_{iV}} > 0$$

Equations (12.2) represent a system of n linear equations in the n variables z_{ij} which implicitly define the individual's demand for shareholdings. It is clear that a high value for β_i goes with a low level of risk aversion, and vice versa. This is also seen from inspection of Figure 12-1: a low risk aversion position (near point B) represents a tangency with a rather steep indifference curve, but the slope of an indifference curve is given by

$$\frac{dV_i}{dE_i} = -\frac{f_{iE}}{f_{iV}} = 2\beta_i$$

12.3. Summing equations (12.2) over i gives

$$\sum_i \sum_k z_{ik}\sigma_{jk} = (\mu_j - rp_j)\sum_i \beta_i$$

The left hand side can be written

$$\sum_k \sigma_{jk}\sum_i z_{ik}$$

which, because of the market clearing conditions

$$\sum_i z_{ik} = 1$$

reduces to

$$\sum_k \sigma_{jk}$$

We have then

$$\sum_k \sigma_{jk} = (\mu_j - rp_j)\sum_i \beta_i$$

and defining

$$R \equiv 1\Big/ \sum_i \beta_i$$

$$b_j \equiv \sum_k \sigma_{jk}$$

we can solve for p_j as

$$p_j = \frac{1}{r}(\mu_j - Rb_j) \tag{12.3}$$

This is the market valuation formula that we referred to earlier.

The structure of this formula is quite easily interpreted. The term Rb_j is a correction term for risk, and the equilibrium value of the firm thus appears as the expected output of the firm less a correction term for risk, the difference being discounted at the risk free interest rate. The correction term for risk itself is the product of two factors, R and b_j. Of these, b_j is the *risk measure* associated with firm j's output and is the sum of the variance of output and the covariances with all other firms. The factor R, on the other hand, is a weighting factor for the firm's risk measure, and is seen to reflect a sort of average strength of risk aversion in the market: the lower the individual β_i, the higher is R. In the models we shall discuss below, the value of R is taken as an exogenously given market characteristic reflecting individuals' preferences. We shall refer to R as the *market risk aversion factor*.

12.4. One further property of equilibrium portfolios will be needed later on. If prices are equilibrium prices, so that

$$\mu_j - rp_j = R\sum_k \sigma_{jk}$$

the optimality conditions (12.2) become

$$\sum_k z_{ik}\sigma_{jk} = \beta_i R \sum_k \sigma_{jk}$$

or

$$\sum_k \sigma_{jk}(z_{ik} - \beta_i R) = 0$$

These equations are clearly always satisfied if $z_{ij} = \beta_i R$ for all j, although other solutions may also exist if the covariance matrix is singular (i.e., if there is linear dependence among output vectors). However, because of the concavity of the preference function, the income vectors corresponding to different solutions must be identical. As far as stochastic properties and preferences are concerned, any equilibrium portfolio can therefore be taken as being perfectly balanced with $z_{ij} = z_i = \beta_i R$ for all j.

We have already, in chapter 8, discussed some aspects of the mean-variance approach to portfolio selection and the assumption of homogeneous expectations. In particular, we observed that any portfolio that is mean-variance efficient also maximizes the expectation of some quadratic utility function. This is because the quadratic is the only utility function whose expectation can be expressed in terms of the mean and variance only of the probability distribution. These, and only these, functions will give an optimal portfolio along the mean-variance efficiency locus. The significance of this in the present context is that quadratic utility functions belong to the linear risk tolerance class which, together with homogeneous expectations, implied distributive efficiency of a competitive stock market. Hence, a model with portfolio selection based on mean-variance efficiency and homogeneous expectations automatically satisfies the conditions for a Pareto-optimal allocation of second-period income among individuals. Therefore, if a stock market satisfying these conditions leads to a Pareto-optimal allocation of investment capital among firms, then the complete allocation is an unconstrained Pareto optimum, so that the question of investment efficiency can be analyzed without explicit consideration of problems of distribution.

13 Stiglitz's Model

13.1. The papers of Jensen and Long [2] and Stiglitz [4], which both contradicted Diamond's conclusion that market determined investment levels would be Pareto-optimal, appeared virtually simultaneously and were apparently written independently of each other. The models differ somewhat in the specification of the investment decisions that firms make, and we shall begin by considering Stiglitz's model and contrast it with Diamond's.

13.2. Like Diamond, Stiglitz assumes production functions with certain separability properties, but of a considerably more general nature, including the possibility of stochastic dependence among different firms' output. Specifically, firm j's output in state θ is written in the form

$$X_j(\theta) = g_j(I_j) + k_j(I_j) F_j(\theta) + m_j(I_j)M(\theta)$$

with the following properties:[a]

$$\mathscr{E}(F_j) = \rho_j$$

$$\mathscr{E}(M) = 0$$

$$\mathrm{Cov}(F_j, F_k) = 0$$

$$\mathrm{Cov}(F_j, M) = 0$$

$$\mathscr{E}(M^2) = 1$$

$$\mathscr{E}(F_j - \rho_j)^2 = \sigma_j^2$$

We see that correlation among the $X_j(\theta)$ is introduced in the simplest possible way through a dependence of a common "market index" $M(\theta)$. In this way the model is quite similar to the "index" or "simplified" model of Sharpe [3]. In addition to the above, we shall also assume

$$g_j(0) = k_j(0) = m_j(0) = 0$$

It follows from this specification that expected return is given by

$$\mu_j = g_j + \rho_j k_j$$

---

[a] These specifications differ slightly from Stiglitz's own, the reason being that we want to be able to treat Diamond's formulation as a special case of Stiglitz's (by setting the functions g_j and m_j equal to zero).

where we have dropped the functional notation. As for the variance we have[b]

$$\sigma_{jj} = \mathcal{E}(X_j - \mu_j)^2$$

$$= \mathcal{E}[k_j^2(F_j - \rho_j)^2 + 2k_jm_j(F_j - \rho_j)M + m_j^2M^2]$$

$$= \sigma_j^2k_j^2 + m_j^2$$

while the proper covariance terms are

$$\sigma_{jk} = \mathcal{E}(X_j - \mu_j)(X_k - \mu_k)$$

$$= \mathcal{E}[k_jk_k(F_j - \rho_j)(F_k - \rho_k) + k_jm_k(F_j - \rho_j)M$$

$$+ k_km_j(F_k - \rho_k)M + m_jm_kM^2]$$

$$= m_jm_k \qquad (k \neq j)$$

The risk measure for firm j is then given by

$$b_j = \sum_k \sigma_{jk} = \sigma_j^2k_j^2 + m_j\sum_k m_k$$

and its market value, according to (12.3), therefore by

$$p_j = \frac{1}{r}\left[g_j + \rho_jk_j - R\left(\sigma_j^2k_j^2 + m_j\sum_k m_k\right)\right] \qquad (13.1)$$

13.3. Stiglitz's basic assumption is now that firms base their calculations of the effect on market value of investment on (13.1), acting as price takers with respect to R and taking the investment levels of other firms as given. To maximize the price per share, the firm will select an investment level such that $dp_j/dI_j = 1$, which leads to the investment rule

$$g_j' + \rho_jk_j' - R\left(2\sigma_j^2k_j'k_j + 2m_j'm_j + m_j'\sum_{k\neq j} m_k\right) = r \qquad (13.2)$$

We note for later reference that since

$$g_j' + \rho_jk_j' = \frac{d\mu_j}{dI_j}$$

$$2\sigma_j^2k_j'k_j + 2m_j'm_j = \frac{d\sigma_{jj}}{dI_j}$$

$$m_j'\sum_{k\neq j} m_k = \sum_{k\neq j}\frac{d\sigma_{jk}}{dI_j}$$

---

[b] Note that σ_j^2 is not the same as σ_{jj}.

we can express (13.2) alternatively as

$$\frac{d\mu_j}{dI_j} - R\left(\frac{d\sigma_{jj}}{dI_j} + \sum_{k\neq j}\frac{d\sigma_{jk}}{dI_j}\right) = r \tag{13.3}$$

13.4. We shall now derive the conditions for a Pareto-optimal allocation of investment capital among firms. The allocation of output to individuals is assumed to be effected by means of stocks and bonds, so that the $Y_i(\theta)$ take the form

$$Y_i(\theta) = \alpha_i + \sum_j \alpha_{ij}X_j(\theta)$$

where the α_i and α_{ij} are restricted by the feasibility conditions

$$\sum_i \alpha_i = rM \tag{13.4}$$

$$\sum_i \alpha_{ij} = 1 \qquad (j = 1, \ldots, n) \tag{13.5}$$

These conditions ensure that we have $\Sigma_i Y_i(\theta) = rM + \Sigma_j X_j(\theta)$ for all θ. In addition we have the first-period feasibility constraint

$$\sum_j I_j + M = S \tag{13.6}$$

where S is exogeneously given.

Individual preference functions are as before given by

$$U_i = f_i(E_i, V_i)$$

where

$$E_i = \alpha_i + \sum_j \alpha_{ij}\mu_j$$

$$= \alpha_i + \sum_j \alpha_{ij}(g_j + \rho_j k_j)$$

$$V_i = \sum_j \sum_k \alpha_{ij}\alpha_{ik}\sigma_{jk}$$

$$= \sum_j \sum_{k\neq j} \alpha_{ij}\alpha_{ik}\sigma_{jk} + \sum_j \alpha_{ij}^2\sigma_{jj}$$

$$= \sum_j \sum_{k\neq j} \alpha_{ij}\alpha_{ik}m_jm_k + \sum_j \alpha_{ij}^2(\sigma_j^2 k_j^2 + m_j^2)$$

$$= \sum_j \alpha_{ij} m_j \sum_{k \neq j} \alpha_{ik} m_k + \sum_j (\alpha_{ij} \sigma_j k_j)^2 + \sum_j \alpha_{ij}^2 m_j^2$$

$$= \sum_j \alpha_{ij} m_j \sum_k \alpha_{ik} m_k + \sum_j (\alpha_{ij} \sigma_j k_j)^2$$

$$= \left(\sum_j \alpha_{ij} m_j \right)^2 + \sum_j (\alpha_{ij} \sigma_j k_j)^2$$

A Pareto-optimal allocation is then an allocation $\{M, I_j, \alpha_i, \alpha_{ij}\}$ that maximizes a positively weighted sum $\Sigma_i k_i U_i$ of individual preference functions, subject to the conditions (13.4) through (13.6).

Associating the Lagrange multipliers λ with (13.4), γ_j with the jth equation in (13.5), and ω with (13.6), the maximand is then

$$L = \sum_i k_i f_i(E_i, V_i) + \lambda \left(rM - \sum_i \alpha_i \right)$$

$$+ \sum_j \gamma_j \left(1 - \sum_i \alpha_{ij} \right) + \omega \left(S - M - \sum_j I_j \right)$$

and the first-order conditions for a maximum are:

$$\frac{\partial L}{\partial M} = \lambda r - \omega = 0 \qquad (13.7)$$

$$\frac{\partial L}{\partial I_j} = \sum_i k_i \left(f_{iE} \frac{\partial E_i}{\partial I_j} + f_{iV} \frac{\partial V_i}{\partial I_j} \right) - \omega$$

$$= \sum_i k_i \left[f_{iE} \alpha_{ij} (g_j' + \rho_j k_j') + f_{iV} \left(2\alpha_{ij}^2 \sigma_j^2 k_j' k_j \right. \right.$$

$$\left. \left. + 2\alpha_{ij} m_j' \sum_k \alpha_{ik} m_k \right) \right] - \omega$$

$$= \sum_i k_i f_{iE} \left[\alpha_{ij} (g_j' + \rho_j k_j') - \frac{\alpha_{ij}}{\beta_i} \left(\alpha_{ij} \sigma_j^2 k_j' k_j + m_j' \sum_k \alpha_{ik} m_k \right) \right] - \omega$$

$$= 0 \qquad (13.8)$$

$$\frac{\partial L}{\partial \alpha_i} = k_i f_{iE} - \lambda = 0 \qquad (13.9)$$

$$\frac{\partial L}{\partial \alpha_{ij}} = k_i \left(f_{iE} \frac{\partial E_i}{\partial \alpha_{ij}} + f_{iV} \frac{\partial V_i}{\partial \alpha_{ij}} \right) - \gamma_j$$

$$= k_i \left[f_{iE} (g_j + \rho_j k_j) + f_{iV} \left(2\alpha_{ij} \sigma_j^2 k_j^2 + 2m_j \sum_k \alpha_{ik} m_k \right) \right] - \gamma_j$$

$$= k_i f_{iE} \left[g_j + \rho_j k_j - \frac{1}{\beta_i} \left(\alpha_{ij} \sigma_j^2 k_j^2 + m_j \sum_k \alpha_{ik} m_k \right) \right] - \gamma_j$$

$$= 0 \tag{13.10}$$

In (13.8) and (13.10) we have used the definition $\beta_i \equiv -f_{iE}/2f_{iV}$ introduced in chapter 12.

The derivation of the conditions for Pareto-optimal investment levels now proceeds as follows. From (13.7) we have $\lambda = \omega/r$, which combined with (13.9) gives

$$k_i f_{iE} = \frac{\omega}{r}$$

Substituting this in (13.8) gives

$$\sum_i \left[\alpha_{ij}(g_j' + \rho_j k_j') - \frac{\alpha_{ij}}{\beta_i} \left(\alpha_{ij} \sigma_j^2 k_j' k_j + m_j' \sum_k \alpha_{ik} m_k \right) \right] = r \tag{13.11}$$

while the same substitution in (13.10) gives

$$g_j + \rho_j k_j - \left(\frac{\alpha_{ij}}{\beta_i} \sigma_j^2 k_j^2 + m_j \sum_k \frac{\alpha_{ik}}{\beta_i} m_k \right) = \frac{r\gamma_j}{\omega} \tag{13.12}$$

The relation (13.12) is to hold for all i, j and is therefore satisfied if and only if

$$\frac{\alpha_{ij}}{\beta_i} = \frac{\alpha_{1j}}{\beta_1}$$

for all i. We must therefore have

$$\alpha_{ij} = \frac{\alpha_{1j}}{\beta_1} \beta_i \tag{13.13}$$

and consequently

$$\sum_i \alpha_{ij} = \frac{\alpha_{1j}}{\beta_1} \sum_i \beta_i = 1$$

so that

$$\frac{\alpha_{1j}}{\beta_1} = R$$

where R by our earlier definition equals $1/\Sigma_i \beta_i$. Substituting back in (13.13) then gives

$$\alpha_{ij} = R\beta_i \qquad (j = 1, \ldots, n)$$

We have already seen that such a condition is satisfied for optimal portfolios in equilibrium. Using this condition in (13.11) then yields the conditions for Pareto-optimal investment levels:

$$g_j' + \rho_j k_j' - R\left(\sigma_j^2 k_j' k_j + m_j' m_j + m_j' \sum_{k \neq j} m_k\right) = r \qquad (13.14)$$

Comparing this condition with the market investment rule (13.2), we see that they are not the same; hence the market rule will not generally lead to a Pareto-optimal allocation of investment. More specifically, the reason for such a misallocation is that the correction term for risk employed by the firm is not what is "should" be relative to (13.14). To see the difference more clearly, we can write (13.14) as

$$\frac{d\mu_j}{dI_j} - R\left(\frac{1}{2}\frac{d\sigma_{jj}}{dI_j} + \sum_{k \neq j} \frac{d\sigma_{jk}}{dI_j}\right) = r$$

Thus, a comparison with (13.2) reveals that the market investment rule places twice as much weight on the effect on its own variance relative to the covariance terms as does the Pareto-optimal investment rule. For a given value of the market risk aversion factor R, this would seem to imply that the market rule would lead to lower investment levels than required for Pareto-optimality. This is in fact a correct conclusion, but we shall have to postpone the analysis of this question until the following chapter.

13.5. To explore the underlying reason for the suboptimality of the market investment rule in Stiglitz's model we shall return to a consideration of Diamond's model. In particular, we want to see what light the mean-variance valuation formula (12.3) can throw on Diamond's proportionality assumption.

Since Diamond's production function is a special case of Stiglitz's obtained by setting both g_j and m_j identically equal to zero, the expression (13.1) for the market value of the firm becomes

$$p_j = \frac{1}{r}(\rho_j k_j - R\sigma_j^2 k_j^2) \qquad (13.15)$$

Suppose now that, in order to keep the probability distribution for return per share invariant to the level of investment, the number of shares outstanding is set equal to k_j as explained in chapter 11. Then (13.15) implies that the price per share is given by

$$\frac{p_j}{n_j} = \frac{p_j}{k_j} = \frac{1}{r}(\rho_j - R\sigma_j^2 k_j) \qquad (13.16)$$

which is seen to be a declining function of k_j, or the number of shares issued. Thus, in contrast to the premise of the proportionality assumption, we obtain a market demand schedule for shares with identical probability distributions for return per share such that the price per share decreases with the number of shares issued. This means that the mean-variance valuation model implies that the firm *cannot* sell an unlimited quantity of identical shares at a fixed price. The market situation can therefore be characterized as one of monopolistic competition among firms.

These monopolistic elements arise simply because (in the absence of perfectly correlated returns) each firm is the sole supplier of shares with its particular probability distribution for return. The important point is now that if each firm takes this monopoly power, as evidenced by the downward sloping demand schedule for its shares, into account, then the resulting investment levels are not Pareto-optimal. If, however, they base their decision making on the (false) assumption of a perfectly elastic demand schedule, Pareto-optimality results.

13.6. This conclusion has an obvious parallel in traditional market theory under certainty. There we know that a profit maximizing producer facing a downward sloping demand schedule will select an output level that is not Pareto-optimal. If, however, he *believes* himself incapable of influencing the price (corresponding to the proportionality assumption) he will select an output level such that price equals marginal cost, and this we know is a requirement for Pareto-optimality. This output is larger than that which would actually maximize his profit, however. To elaborate, write the producer's profit function as

$$\Pi = S - C(x)$$

where S is sales revenue and $C(x)$ cost as a function of output x. If now the producer believes that revenue is proportional to output, i.e., $S = \alpha x$, he will find it in his interest to choose x such that $C'(x) = \alpha$. Since the proportionality factor is not known, however, this condition must be expressed in the form

$$C'(x) = \frac{S}{x}$$

This condition can be used (ex post) to confirm that the "optimal" x has been chosen. If S is in fact given by $S = xf(x)$, where $f(x)$ is price as a function of output, the decision rule becomes $C'(x) = f(x)$, i.e., price equals marginal cost.

Returning to our investment model, we observe that for the case of decomposable production functions the market investment rule (13.2) becomes

$$\rho_j k_j' - 2R\sigma_j^2 k_j' k_j = r$$

while the condition (13.14) for Pareto optimality reduces to

$$\rho_j k_j' - R\sigma_j^2 k_j' k_j = r \tag{13.17}$$

In Diamond's model we wrote the condition for an optimal investment level in the form (11.3), i.e., as

$$\frac{k_j'}{k_j} p_j = 1$$

We now see that if market value is in fact given by (13.15), this condition becomes

$$\frac{k_j'}{k_j} \cdot \frac{1}{r} (\rho_j k_j - R\sigma_j^2 k_j^2) = 1$$

or

$$\rho_j k_j' - R\sigma_j^2 k_j' k_j = r$$

and is thus identical with (13.17). This demonstrates directly the Pareto-optimality of Diamond's investment rule.

13.7. In the general case of nondecomposable production functions (where the proportionality assumption is just meaningless), the assumption that firms act as price takers with respect to the market risk aversion factor R seems to be the only sensible alternative—at least within the context of a mean-variance valuation model. Accepting that might lead us to the conclusion that there is something "wrong" with share value maximization as a company objective. To put the whole blame for the inefficiency of the market allocation on the objective of maximizing the market value of the firm's shares is not really fair, however. The competitive situation in the market such as that specified in Stiglitz's model clearly also plays a significant part.

It is nevertheless natural to ask the question: If share price maximization leads to investment decisions that are not Pareto-optimal, can this objective possibly be in the shareholders' best interest? The answer to this question was—at least in part—provided by the paper by Ekern and Wilson [1] on stockholder agreement with company decisions. Since the analysis of this question throws additional light on the Diamond and Stiglitz models, we shall present it before proceeding to other models based on mean-variance valuation.

References

1. Ekern, S., and R. Wilson, "On the Theory of the Firm in an Econo-

my with Incomplete Markets," *Bell Journal of Economics and Management Science*, 1974, pp. 171-180.

2. Jensen, M., and J. Long, "Corporate Investment under Uncertainty and Pareto Optimality in the Capital Markets," *Bell Journal of Economics and Management Science*, 1972, pp. 151-174.

3. Sharpe, W.F., "A Simplified Model for Portfolio Analysis," *Management Science*, 1963, pp. 277-293.

4. Stiglitz, J.E., "On the Optimality of the Stock Market Allocation of Investment," *Quarterly Journal of Economics*, 1972, pp. 25-60.

14 Stockholder Agreement

14.1. Ekern and Wilson [1] take as starting point a market situation which Leland [2] has termed a *financial equilibrium*. By this we mean a situation where firms have somehow chosen investment levels I_j with corresponding output vectors $X_j(\theta)$, and individual consumers have chosen stock-bond portfolios that are optimal (for given, but arbitrary, preferences, probability beliefs, and initial resources) relative to these investment levels. The market clearing conditions are satisfied, so the ruling share prices are equilibrium prices—again relative to the given investment levels. However, no assumptions are made about whether or not the investment levels themselves are optimal by any choice criterion.

The idea is now to evaluate the desirability—in terms of changes in individual expected utilities—of a marginal change in a given firm's level of investment. The main purpose of this analysis is to explore conditions under which the firm's shareholders will unanimously agree on the desirability of such a change. The rationale behind this is clearly that if such unanimity prevails, one can dispense with a choice criterion such as value maximization entirely and just ask any shareholder what he thinks should be done. Or, if the firm's manager is himself a stockholder (which is often the case), he can simply be guided by his own preferences.

14.2. In the formulation of the effect of changing the level of investment of firm j, Ekern and Wilson do not specify how this change is financed. In fact, with $Y_i(\theta)$ given by

$$Y_i(\theta) = rm_i + \sum_j z_{ij} X_j(\theta)$$

they write the change in individual i's income as

$$\frac{dY_i(\theta)}{dI_j} = z_{ij} \frac{dX_j(\theta)}{dI_j}$$

disregarding the reallocation of resources that a change in I_j necessarily requires. To set this right we shall here assume that individuals contribute to the change in I_j, dI_j, in proportion to their shareholdings in the firm, and that they finance this contribution by a reduction in their riskless investment.[a] We thus have $dm_i = -z_{ij}dI_j$; the change in $Y_i(\theta)$ is then

---

[a] Alternatively, we could have specified an offsetting change in first-period consumption, but this would not have altered the change in expected utility.

$$\frac{dY_i(\theta)}{dI_j} = z_{ij}\left(\frac{dX_j(\theta)}{dI_j} - r\right)$$

and the changes in expected utility accordingly

$$\frac{dU_i}{dI_j} = \mathcal{E}_i\left[u_i'(Y_i)\frac{dY_i}{dI_j}\right]$$

$$= z_{ij}\mathcal{E}_i\left[u_i'(Y_i)\left(\frac{dX_j}{dI_j} - r\right)\right] \qquad (14.1)$$

The first-order conditions for the optimal z_{ij} are given by (11.1).

14.3. The question of unanimity is now the question of finding conditions which, in the absence of complete markets, are such that the derivatives (14.1) are all of the same sign. As we have seen, the lack of complete markets means that the set of attainable income vectors $Y_i(\theta)$ is restricted to a linear subspace of the complete s-dimensional income space. Ekern and Wilson's unanimity proposition states that a sufficient condition for unanimity is that the production function is such that the change in the firm's output vector $X_j(\theta)$ caused by the change in I_j can be expressed as some linear combination of the existing output vectors, i.e.,

$$\frac{dX_j(\theta)}{dI_j} = \sum_k h_{jk}X_k(\theta) + h_{j0}r \qquad (14.2)$$

If the production function satisfies this condition it is said to have the *spanning* property.

To show that this condition implies unanimity, we substitute in (14.1) to get

$$\frac{dU_i}{dI_j} = z_{ij}\mathcal{E}_i\left[u_i'(Y_i)\left(\sum_k h_{jk}X_k + r(h_{j0} - 1)\right)\right]$$

$$= z_{ij}\left\{\sum_k h_{jk}\mathcal{E}_i[u_i'(Y_i)X_k] + r(h_{j0} - 1)\mathcal{E}_i[u_i'(Y_i)]\right\}$$

From the optimality conditions (11.1) we have

$$\mathcal{E}_i[u_i'(Y_i)X_k] = rp_k\mathcal{E}_i[u_i'(Y_i)]$$

hence

$$\frac{dU_i}{dI_j} = z_{ij}r\mathcal{E}_i[u_i'(Y_i)]\left(\sum_k h_{jk}p_k + h_{j0} - 1\right)$$

Since $\mathcal{E}_i[u_i'(Y_i)] > 0$ and the last factor is the same for all individuals, this derivative will be of the same sign for all individuals who hold a positive fraction of the firm's shares. Hence the unanimity proposition follows: all these individuals will agree that I_j should be increased, stay the same, or be reduced, as the factor

$$G_j \equiv \sum_k h_{jk}p_k + h_{j0} - 1 \qquad (14.3)$$

is positive, zero, or negative. Obviously, an individual who has chosen to take a short position in the firm's shares will prefer exactly the opposite. This possibility may raise a minor problem as far as welfare implications are concerned: although a company's management can safely choose to ignore the preferences of those individuals with $z_{ij} < 0$, it is less evident that we should be entitled to do so from a social welfare point of view. Of course, no problem arises if we assume homogeneous expectations, since in that case the z_{ij} must be nonnegative for all individuals. Furthermore, if the factor $G_j = 0$, the signs of the z_{ij} make no difference and the given investment levels are clearly Pareto-optimal. If, however, the z_{ij} have different signs for different individuals and $G_j \neq 0$, then we have a situation that is Pareto-optimal (since the dU_i/dI_j are not all of the same sign) but where nevertheless actual shareholders may unanimously support a change in the allocation.

14.4. The economic significance of the spanning property and the intuitive meaning of the unanimity proposition can be explained as follows. At the original equilibrium, individual i holds a portfolio $\{m_i, z_{ik}\}$ with a return distribution

$$Y_i(\theta) = rm_i + \sum_k z_{ik}X_k(\theta)$$

The market value of this portfolio is

$$W_i = m_i + \sum_k z_{ik}p_k$$

If $X_j(\theta)$ is changed in such a way that (14.2) is satisfied, then it is possible for the individual to adjust his original portfolio so as to obtain exactly the same income vector as he had before. That is, portfolio adjustments $\{dm_i, dz_{ik}\}$ i exist such that $dY_i(\theta) = 0$ for all θ; they therefore satisfy

$$dY_i(\theta) = rdm_i + z_{ij}dX_j(\theta) + \sum_k dz_{ik}X_k(\theta)$$

$$= rdm_i + z_{ij}\left[\sum_k h_{jk}X_k(\theta) + h_{j0}r\right]dI_j + \sum_k dz_{ik}X_k(\theta)$$

$$= r(dm_i + z_{ij}h_{j0}dI_j) + \sum_k (dz_{ik} + z_{ij}h_{jk}\,dI_j)X_k(\theta)$$

$$= 0 \qquad (\theta = 1, \ldots, s)$$

Since we assume incomplete markets (fewer linearly independent securities than states of the world), these conditions are satisfied if and only if

$$dm_i = -z_{ij}h_{j0}dI_j$$

$$dz_{ik} = -z_{ij}h_{jk}dI_j$$

The net proceeds from these sales and/or purchases of securities equal

$$-dW_i = -\left(dm_i + \sum_k dz_{ik}p_k\right)$$

$$= z_{ij}\left(\sum_k h_{jk}p_k + h_{j0}\right)dI_j$$

which may be positive or negative. On the other hand, the contribution required from the individual to effect the change in $X_j(\theta)$ is $z_{ij}dI_j$ (which may also be positive or negative). The question is now: Is it possible for the individual to contribute to the change in I_j, then adjust his portfolio so as to obtain the same income vector as before, and come out with a net profit? If yes, he would clearly be in a better position than before and will therefore endorse the proposed change. The condition is clearly that

$$z_{ij}\left(\sum_k h_{jk}p_k + h_{j0}\right)dI_j \geq z_{ij}dI_j$$

or

$$z_{ij}G_jdI_j \geq 0$$

Assuming $z_{ij} > 0$, this holds if and only if G_j and dI_j are of the same sign. But this is precisely the result we derived above.

14.5. We now apply the condition for unanimity to the models of Diamond and Stiglitz. Diamond's decomposable production function has the property

$$\frac{dX_j}{dI_j} = \frac{k_j'}{k_j}X_j(\theta)$$

and therefore clearly satisfies (14.2) with $h_{jj} = k_j'/k_j$ and $h_{jk} = 0$ ($k \neq j$), $h_{j0} = 0$. The factor G_j is then

$$G_j = \frac{k_j'}{k_j}p_j - 1$$

and we now observe that if the firm has in fact based its investment decision on the proportionality assumption and thus selected a level of investment satisfying (11.3), then G_j, and so also dU_i/dI_j, equals zero. We already know that (11.3) implies Pareto-optimality; we have now confirmed that in this case shareholders agree that no change in investment levels should be undertaken.

Consider next Stiglitz's model with the simplifying assumption of uncorrelated outputs[b] ($m_j = 0$); the production function was then given by

$$X_j(\theta) = g_j(I_j) + k_j(I_j) F_j(\theta)$$

and hence

$$\frac{dX_j(\theta)}{dI_j} = g_j' + k_j' F_j(\theta)$$

$$= g_j' + k_j' \frac{X_j(\theta) - g_j}{k_j}$$

$$= \frac{k_j'}{k_j} X_j(\theta) + \left(g_j' - \frac{k_j'}{k_j} g_j \right)$$

We see that also in this case is the requirement (14.2) satisfied with $h_{jj} = k_j'/k_j$, $h_{jk} = 0$ for $k \neq j$, and

$$h_{j0} = \frac{1}{r} \left(g_j' - \frac{k_j'}{k_j} g_j \right)$$

The factor G_j is then given by

$$G_j = \frac{k_j'}{k_j} p_j + \frac{1}{r} \left(g_j' - \frac{k_j'}{k_j} g_j \right) - 1$$

$$= \frac{1}{r} \left[g_j' - r - \frac{k_j'}{k_j} (g_j - rp_j) \right]$$

If now in fact the value of the firm is given by (12.3) (with the $m_j = 0$) as

$$p_j = \frac{1}{r} (g_j + \rho_j k_j - R\sigma_j^2 k_j^2)$$

then

$$g_j - rp_j = R\sigma_j^2 k_j^2 - \rho_j k_j$$

and G_j becomes

$$G_j = \frac{1}{r} (g_j' + \rho_j k_j' - R\sigma_j^2 k_j' k_j - r)$$

---

[b] If we make the (plausible) assumption that the "market index" $M(\theta)$ represents a linear combination of the $X_k(\theta)$, the analysis goes through but is rather messy.

The condition for Pareto-optimality was for this model given by (13.14), i.e.,

$$g_j' + \rho_j k_j' - R\sigma_j^2 k_j' k_j = r$$

If this is satisfied we clearly again find $G_j = 0$. Suppose, on the other hand, that the investment level satisfies the value maximizing condition (13.2):

$$g_j' + \rho_j k_j' - 2R\sigma_j^2 k_j' k_j = r$$

so that G_j becomes

$$G_j = \frac{1}{r} R\sigma_j^2 k_j' k_j$$

By assumption, $k_j(0) = 0$, and if k_j is a monotonic function, k_j' and k_j must clearly be of the same sign which implies $G_j > 0$. This seems an eminently reasonable property of the production function; indeed, it is implied by the assumption that the variance (in absolute terms) increases with the level of investment: since $\sigma_{jj} = \sigma_j^2 k_j^2$, $d\sigma_{jj}/dI_j = 2\sigma_j^2 k_j' k_j$. In this case, all shareholders will agree that the level of investment should be increased. This substantiates the hypothesis that the value maximizing level of investment is smaller than that required for Pareto-optimality.

The rationale behind the assumption of share price maximization as an appropriate objective for the firm has been the natural belief that this objective is in accordance with the shareholders' best interests. The analysis above, however, clearly brings out a potential conflict between share price maximization and stockholder interests. We shall have more to say on the nature of such a conflict later on.

References

1. Ekern, S., and R. Wilson, "On the Theory of the Firm in an Economy with Incomplete Markets," *Bell Journal of Economics and Management Science*, 1974, pp. 171-180.

2. Leland, H.E., "Production Theory and the Stock Market," *Bell Journal of Economics and Management Science*, 1974, pp. 145-170.

15

Exclusive versus Competitive Investment

15.1. In this chapter we give a reconstruction of the model presented by Jensen and Long [1] and the reformulation of this model suggested by Merton and Subrahmanyam [2], which highlights the nature of competition (or lack thereof) in the earlier models.

Jensen and Long's analysis has points in common with both Stiglitz and Ekern and Wilson. Like Stiglitz, they assume that company values are determined in accordance with the mean-variance valuation formula (12.3), but otherwise their analytical approach is different from that followed by Stiglitz. Like Ekern and Wilson, they take as their starting point a situation of financial equilibrium and explore the consequences of altering the given allocation of investment capital. Unlike Ekern and Wilson, however, they do not consider a change in the level of input to one of the originally given production functions, but rather a reallocation of investment capital into a "new" investment opportunity that becomes available. Thus, they want to examine the welfare implications of the market's adaptation to an expansion of the available investment opportunities. An example might be the opportunity facing Du Pont at the end of World War II after the development (and patenting) of nylon.

Return on investment in the new opportunity is assumed to be of the stochastically constant returns to scale type, i.e., a second-period output of $Z(\theta)$ per unit (dollar) of investment. We denote the mean of Z by μ_Z, its variance by σ_Z^2 and its covariance with existing return distributions X_k by σ_{Zk} ($k = 1, \ldots, n$).

As in Ekern and Wilson's model we shall specify financing of the new investment through a reduction in the amount of riskless investment.[a] We then start by deriving the amount of investment in the new project that would be considered optimal from a social welfare point of view.

15.2. In the original situation, individual i holds a portfolio $\{m_i^*, z_{ik}^*\}$; under the assumptions of the mean-variance model equilibrium portfolios are perfectly balanced (or have probability distributions for return identical with such portfolios), i.e., $z_{ik}^* = z_i^*$ for all k. The return from such a portfolio is therefore

$$Y_i^*(\theta) = rm_i^* + z_i^* \sum_k X_k(\theta)$$

---

[a] Again, specifying financing through reduced first-period consumption would give identical conclusions.

133

with mean and variance

$$E_i^* = rm_i^* + z_i^* \sum_k \mu_k$$

$$V_i^* = (z_i^*)^2 \sum_j \sum_k \sigma_{jk}$$

We now propose to invest an amount I in the new project such that all individuals contribute in proportion to their original shares of the risky industry. Thus the amount contributed by individual i is $z_i^* I$, in return for which he will be entitled to receive an extra (random) amount $z_i^* I Z(\theta)$ in the second period. His income would in this way be changed to

$$Y_i(\theta) = r(m_i^* - z_i^* I) + z_i^* \left[\sum_k X_k(\theta) + IZ(\theta) \right]$$

$$= \left[rm_i^* + z_i^* \sum_k X_k(\theta) \right] + z_i^* I[Z(\theta) - r]$$

$$= Y_i^*(\theta) + z_i^* I[Z(\theta) - r]$$

so that the new mean and variance become

$$E_i = E_i^* + z_i^* I(\mu_Z - r)$$

$$V_i = \mathcal{E}(Y_i - E_i)^2$$

$$= \mathcal{E}[Y_i^* - E_i^* + z_i^* I(Z - \mu_Z)]^2$$

$$= \mathcal{E}(Y_i^* - E_i^*)^2 + 2z_i^* I \mathcal{E}(Y_i^* - E_i^*)(Z - \mu_Z) + (z_i^*)^2 I^2 \mathcal{E}(Z - \mu_Z)^2$$

Since

$$Y_i^* - E_i^* = z_i^* \sum_k (X_k - \mu_k)$$

the expectation in the middle term equals

$$z_i^* \sum_k \sigma_{Zk}$$

hence

$$V_i = V_i^* + 2(z_i^*)^2 I \sum_k \sigma_{Zk} + (z_i^* I)^2 \sigma_Z^2$$

Each individual is now asked how much (if anything) he thinks should be invested, given the particular arrangement of financing and distribution as specified. To answer this, the individual will evaluate the effect on his preference function $U_i = f_i(E_i, V_i)$, i.e., the derivative

$$\frac{dU_i}{dI} = f_{iE}\frac{dE_i}{dI} + f_{iV}\frac{dV_i}{dI}$$

$$= f_{iE}z_i^*(\mu_z - r) + 2f_{iV}(z_i^*)^2\left(\sum_k \sigma_{jk} + I\sigma_z^2\right)$$

$$= z_i^*f_{iE}\left[\mu_z - r + \frac{2f_{iV}}{f_{iE}}z_i^*\left(\sum_k \sigma_{Zk} + I\sigma_z^2\right)\right]$$

$$= z_i^*f_{iE}\left[\mu_z - r - \frac{z_i^*}{\beta_i}\left(\sum_k \sigma_{Zk} + I\sigma_z^2\right)\right]$$

Since in equilibrium the optimal z_i^* satisfies $z_i^* = \beta_i R$, this can be written

$$\frac{dU_i}{dI} = z_i^*f_{iE}\left[\mu_z - r - R\left(\sum_k \sigma_{Zk} + I\sigma_z^2\right)\right]$$

In this expression, the bracketed term is the same for all individuals, and since $z_i^*f_{iE} > 0$, they will all agree on the optimal value of I. No investment should be undertaken unless

$$\left.\frac{dU_i}{dI}\right|_{I=0} > 0$$

i.e., if

$$\mu_z - R\sum_k \sigma_{Zk} > r \tag{15.1}$$

and, assuming this condition to be satisfied, the optimal level of investment is determined by the condition $dU_i/dI = 0$, i.e.,

$$\mu_z - R\left(\sum_k \sigma_{Zk} + I\sigma_z^2\right) = r \tag{15.2}$$

This condition Jensen and Long refer to as their "social welfare" criterion for investment.

It should be noted that this criterion is derived on the assumption that individuals will hold the same proportion of total risky output before and after the introduction of the new opportunity. In fact, of course, the equilibrium values of the z_i would generally change. As a description of the actual effect on expected utility, the criterion can therefore be taken only as an approximation in the neighborhood of the original equilibrium position, and we have no way of knowing whether such an approximation is acceptable or not. As an extreme possibility, the new opportunity might be so favorable that it would (or should) completely wipe out existing firms.

15.3. Jensen and Long now consider the situation where investment in the new project is to be undertaken by some particular firm, say firm j, whose original output vector we now distinguish as $X_j^*(\theta)$. The firm raises an amount I_j from the outside; we must presume that this amount also represents a reduction in riskless investment or first-period consumption. The firm's second-period output will then change to

$$X_j(\theta) = X_j^*(\theta) + I_j Z(\theta)$$

and therefore the mean, variance, and covariance terms to

$$\mu_j = \mu_j^* + I_j \mu_z$$

$$
\begin{aligned}
\sigma_{jj} &= \mathcal{E}(X_j - \mu_j)^2 \\
&= \mathcal{E}[(X_j^* - \mu_j^*) + I_j(Z - \mu_z)]^2 \\
&= \mathcal{E}(X_j^* - \mu_j^*)^2 + 2I_j\mathcal{E}(X_j^* - \mu_j^*)(Z - \mu_z) + I_j^2\mathcal{E}(Z - \mu_z)^2 \\
&= \sigma_{jj}^* + 2I_j\sigma_{zj} + I_j^2\sigma_z^2
\end{aligned}
$$

and, for $k \neq j$,

$$
\begin{aligned}
\sigma_{jk} &= \mathcal{E}(X_j - \mu_j)(X_k - \mu_k) \\
&= \mathcal{E}(X_j^* - \mu_j^*)(X_k - \mu_k) + I_j\mathcal{E}(Z - \mu_z)(X_k - \mu_k) \\
&= \sigma_{jk}^* + I_j\sigma_{zk}
\end{aligned}
$$

Note that, by assumption, X_k is unchanged for $k \neq j$. With this, the new risk measure for firm j becomes

$$
\begin{aligned}
b_j &= \sigma_{jj} + \sum_{k\neq j}\sigma_{jk} \\
&= \sigma_{jj}^* + 2I_j\sigma_{zj} + I_j^2\sigma_z^2 + \sum_{k\neq j}(\sigma_{jk}^* + I_j\sigma_{zk}) \\
&= b_j^* + I_j\left(2\sigma_{zj} + \sum_{k\neq j}\sigma_{zk}\right) + I_j^2\sigma_z^2
\end{aligned}
$$

The firm will invest only if it calculates that its market value will rise by more than the amount of investment; with market value given by (12.3) the net increase is given by

$$\frac{dp_j}{dI_j} - 1 = \frac{1}{r}\left[\mu_z - R\left(2\sigma_{zj} + 2I_j\sigma_z^2 + \sum_{k\neq j}\sigma_{zk}\right)\right] - 1$$

Thus, no investment will be undertaken unless

$$\mu_Z - R\left(2\sigma_{Zj} + \sum_{k \neq j}\sigma_{Zk}\right) > r \qquad (15.3)$$

and, assuming (15.3) to be satisfied, the optimal level of investment is determined by the condition

$$\mu_Z - R\left(2\sigma_{Zj} + 2I_j\sigma_Z^2 + \sum_{k \neq j}\sigma_{Zk}\right) = r \qquad (15.4)$$

This represents Jensen and Long's "corporate" investment criterion.

15.4. Comparing first the "marginal" conditions (15.1) and (15.3) for any investment at all in the new project, we see that unless the project's return is uncorrelated with the company's preinvestment return ($\sigma_{Zj} = 0$), the corporate criterion is different from the welfare maximizing criterion. If $\sigma_{Zj} > 0$, the corporate criterion is stricter in the sense that there might exist projects with return distributions such that the project would be rejected by the firm while passing the welfare maximizing criterion. If $\sigma_{Zj} < 0$, the converse is true. Second, unless $\sigma_{Zj} = \sigma_{Zk}$ for all j, k, the corporate criterion is different for different firms, whereas (15.1) implies that it is a matter of indifference which firm undertakes the project.

The more interesting comparison, however, is probably of the investment rules (15.2) and (15.4), and particularly their relationship to the investment rules (13.2) and (13.14) of Stiglitz's model. Here we find that despite the dissimilarity of the two approaches, the conclusions we can draw from the models are very much the same. In interpreting these conclusions, however, we have to keep in mind that whereas Stiglitz's investment rules determine the overall activity level for each firm, Jensen and Long's investment rules are concerned only with the level of investment in the "new" project (as seen either from individuals' or from some particular firm's point of view), given the activity levels of existing firms.

To bring out the formal correspondence between the models, note that in Jensen and Long's formulation we have

$$\frac{d\mu_j}{dI_j} = \mu_Z$$

$$\frac{d\sigma_{jj}}{dI_j} = 2\sigma_{Zj} + 2I_j\sigma_Z^2$$

$$\frac{d\sigma_{jk}}{dI_j} = \sigma_{Zk} \qquad (k \neq j)$$

Therefore, the investment rules (15.2) and (15.4) can alternatively be expressed as, respectively,

$$\frac{d\mu_j}{dI_j} - R\left(\frac{1}{2}\frac{d\sigma_{jj}}{dI_j} + \sum_{k\neq j}\frac{d\sigma_{jk}}{dI_j}\right) = r$$

and

$$\frac{d\mu_j}{dI_j} - R\left(\frac{d\sigma_{jj}}{dI_j} + \sum_{k\neq j}\frac{d\sigma_{jk}}{dI_j}\right) = r$$

In this form we recognize the rules as formally indentical with those of Stiglitz. Thus, also here the criterion derived from share price maximization places twice as much weight on the effect on the own-variance as it should from a social welfare point of view.

15.5. We have previously explained the lack of Pareto-optimality resulting from decision rules designed to maximize share prices in terms of certain kinds of monopolistic elements manifesting themselves in a less than perfectly elastic demand for a firm's shares. The source of such monopolistic elements should by now be getting clear, and was made quite explicit in the paper by Merton and Subrahmanyam. They point out that Jensen and Long's corporate investment criterion—just as Stiglitz's market investment rule—is derived on the assumption that the investing firm has an *exclusive right* to invest in the project (or production function) under consideration. With such monopolistic exclusion built into the model, it is really not surprising that the resulting market allocation is not Pareto-optimal.

Merton and Subrahmanyam argue, however, that this assumption is inconsistent with what we mean (or should mean) by a competitive allocation, and suggest a modification more in line with the usual concept of perfect competition. Their paper builds directly on the Jensen and Long model and retains all of their assumptions with the important exception that *all* firms are free to invest in the new project. Such a project could be thought of as a new market opening up, such as the market for diet soda or radial tires or oral contraceptives, to give some recent examples. Whether such a specification is empirically more relevant than one where investment opportunities are tied to individual firms is clearly an open question. Nevertheless, its obvious theoretical relevance lies in the possibility it affords of defining more precisely the notion of perfect competition.

15.6. If $X_j^*(\theta)$ was the original output vector of firm j, it will now change to $X_j(\theta) = X_j^*(\theta) + I_j Z(\theta)$ for *every* firm. The new mean and variance-covariance terms are then

$$\mu_j = \mu_j^* + I_j\mu_Z$$

and

$$\sigma_{jk} = \mathcal{E}(X_j - \mu_j)(X_k - \mu_k)$$

$$= \mathcal{E}[(X_j^* - \mu_j^*) + I_j(Z - \mu_Z)][(X_k^* - \mu_k^*) + I_i(Z - \mu_Z)]$$

$$= \mathcal{E}(X_j^* - \mu_j^*)(X_k^* - \mu_k^*) + I_j\mathcal{E}(Z - \mu_Z)(X_k^* - \mu_k^*)$$

$$+ I_k\mathcal{E}(Z - \mu_Z)(X_j^* - \mu_j^*) + I_jI_k\mathcal{E}(Z - \mu_Z)^2$$

$$= \sigma_{jk}^* + I_j\sigma_{Zk} + I_k\sigma_{Zj} + I_jI_k\sigma_Z^2$$

so that the new risk measure for firm j becomes

$$b_j = \sum_k \sigma_{jk}$$

$$= \sum_k \sigma_{jk}^* + I_j\sum_k \sigma_{Zk} + \sigma_{Zj}\sum_k I_k + I_j\sigma_Z^2\sum_k I_k$$

$$= b_j^* + I\sigma_{Zj} + I_j\left(I\sigma_Z^2 + \sum_k \sigma_{Zk}\right)$$

where $I \equiv \Sigma_k I_k$ is aggregate investment (including that of firm j) in the new project.

Write $p_j(I_j, I)$ for the value of firm j when its own level of investment is I_j and the aggregate level of investment is I. Thus,

$$p_j(I_j, I) = \frac{1}{r}\left\{\mu_j^* + I_j\mu_Z - R\left[b_j^* + I\sigma_{Zj} + I_j\left(I\sigma_Z^2 + \sum_k \sigma_{Zk}\right)\right]\right\}$$

and

$$p_j(0, I) = \frac{1}{r}[\mu_j^* - R(b_j^* + I\sigma_{Zj})]$$

We can now write $p_j(I_j, I)$ in an extremely useful form, namely

$$p_j(I_j, I) = p_j(0, I) + g(I)I_j \tag{15.5}$$

where

$$g(I) = \frac{1}{r}\left[\mu_Z - R\left(I\sigma_Z^2 + \sum_k \sigma_{Zk}\right)\right]$$

To interpret (15.5), note that $p_j(0, I)$ is the value of the firm if it itself had invested nothing in the new project, given an aggregate investment level of I. The second term, $g(I)I_j$, is therefore the incremental value of the firm from its interest in the new project; thus $g(I)$ is the incremental value per unit of investment, and is the same for all firms.

Merton and Subrahmanyam now argue that the appropriate description of the firm as an atomistic price taker is that it considers $p_j(0, I)$ and $g(I)$ as constants with respect to its own choice of I_j.

At first, this admittedly looks like an inconsistency or mathematical error, and, strictly speaking, it clearly is. However, it should be realized that it is precisely in this way we define atomistic price taking (or perfect competition) in conventional market theory. To elaborate, suppose we have a market with several producers supplying the same commodity in quantities x_j; producer j's sales revenue is then

$$S_j = p(x)x_j$$

where $x = \Sigma_k x_k$ is aggregate supply and $p(x)$ the market price depending only on aggregate supply. Now, assuming perfect competition, we proceed by writing

$$\frac{dS_j}{dx_j} = p(x) \tag{15.6}$$

although this clearly is mathematically "wrong." Strictly speaking, the derivative is

$$\frac{dS_j}{dx_j} = p(x) + p'(x)x_j$$

$$= p(x) \left(1 - \eta\frac{x_j}{x}\right) \tag{15.7}$$

where $\eta = -p'(x)x/p(x)$ is the elasticity of the market demand schedule. We rationalize (15.6), however, by saying that atomistic competition means that x_j is so small relative to x that the factor in parentheses in (15.7) "effectively" equals unity.

In the same way, if we want perfect competition in our model of investment allocation to have the same meaning as elsewhere in economics, it follows that we must specify the firm as a price taker with respect to $p_j(0, I)$ and $g(I)$, i.e., it considers these as prices that depend only on the aggregate amount of investment in the new project, the effect on which of its own decision it regards as negligible. Alternatively, we can invoke the assumption of free entry, in which case the firm knows that if it itself chooses not to participate, some other firm will enter the market and bring the aggregate level of investment to its equilibrium value.

15.7. Under this assumption, the firm will calculate the increase in its market value from investing the amount I_j simply as

$$p_j(I_j, I) - p_j(0, I) = g(I)I_j$$

i.e., as proportional to the amount of investment. Note that, although similar, this is not really the same kind of relationship as Diamond's proportionality assumption. Here we are concerned with a number of different firms competitively engaged in the same type of activity, while Diamond's model was concerned with monopoly investment by the individual firm. However, as we now show, the implication of the proportionality relation is quite similar, namely, that the resulting aggregate level of investment is Pareto-optimal.

The firm will assume that its share price will increase whenever $g(I)I_j$ is greater than the amount of investment. Therefore, if $g(I) > 1$, every firm will want to expand its investment indefinitely, but this will cause $g(I)$ to fall [note that $g'(I) < 0$]. If on the other hand $g(I) < 1$, firms will want to contract investment and thus cause $g(I)$ to rise. As a consequence, the only value of $g(I)$ consistent with equilibrium is $g(I) = 1$, or

$$\mu_z - R\left(I\sigma_z^2 + \sum_k \sigma_{zk}\right) = r \tag{15.8}$$

But this we see is precisely the same as the condition (15.2) for Pareto-optimality. Thus, by invoking the appropriate competitive assumptions, Merton and Subrahmanyam are able to establish results corresponding to that of traditional general equilibrium and welfare theory.

Note that because of the constant returns to scale of the new project, while the aggregate amount of investment is determinate, individual firms' investment levels (and the number of firms actually engaged in the activity) are not. Also this result has an exact counterpart in conventional market theory: in a commodity market aggregate output must be such that the corresponding market price equals marginal cost, while individual producers' output levels are indeterminate.

As indicated, the significance of Merton and Subrahmanyam's analysis is that it clarifies the role of possible sources of nonoptimality of a market allocation. The model and its implications thus go a long way towards bringing the theory of optimal investment under uncertainty back into the mainstream of welfare economics.

Even so, some interesting questions still remain unresolved. These are mainly concerned with the potential conflict between company objectives and stockholder preferences, with conflicting interests among the stockholders themselves, and some mechanisms for resolving such conflicts. We turn to an examination of these problems in the last chapter.

References

1. Jensen, M., and J. Long, "Corporate Investment under Uncertain-

ty and Pareto Optimality in the Capital Markets," *Bell Journal of Economics and Management Science*, 1972, pp. 151-174.

2. Merton, R.C., and M.G. Subrahmanyam, "The Optimality of a Competitive Stock Market," *Bell Journal of Economics and Management Science*, 1974, pp. 145-170.

16 Stockholder Disagreement

16.1. Given that exclusive investment rights exist, Ekern and Wilson's analysis clearly demonstrates the possibility of conflict between shareholders' interests and the objective of share price maximization. This possibility is obviously of interest quite apart from questions of Pareto-optimality. Now, if share price maximization is not generally in the shareholders' best interest, then there must be something wrong with what we may refer to as the take-over argument in favor of share price maximization. What this argument says is, somewhat loosely, that if management pursues a policy that does not maximize the share price, then it is possible for someone (call him the raider) to acquire a controlling interest in the firm, change the policy, and subsequently sell his shares at a profit. The plausibility of this argument has also come under attack lately.

In economic literature, the phenomenon of take-over bids or similar mechanisms does not seem to have been examined in any detail from a theoretical point of view. It is noteworthy, however, that textbooks in finance usually present a take-over bid as a substitute for a stockholder meeting or a proxy fight. Such a view appears to be based on a misconception of the circumstances under which each of these various mechanisms might be set in motion.

Why should a stockholder be willing to sell his shares to the raider? If he believes the raider's claim that another policy exists that would result in a higher price per share, and furthermore believes that the raider will be successful in carrying out his designs, then it would certainly be a very stupid thing to part with his shares. Consequently, we have the somewhat paradoxical conclusion that in order for a take-over bid to be successful, there must be a sufficient number of shareholders who disagree that a policy such as that proposed by the raider exists. But if that is the case, there would not have been a basis for a stockholders' meeting or a proxy fight to change the policy. Thus, a take-over bid and a stockholders' meeting cannot be substitutes under the same set of circumstances. We note however, that stock acquisition and proxy holdings may act as complements: the raider buys shares from the people who don't believe him and obtains proxies from those who do.

16.2. Some discussion of these problems have been offered, among others, by King [1] and Leland [2]. Both are concerned with a firm for which

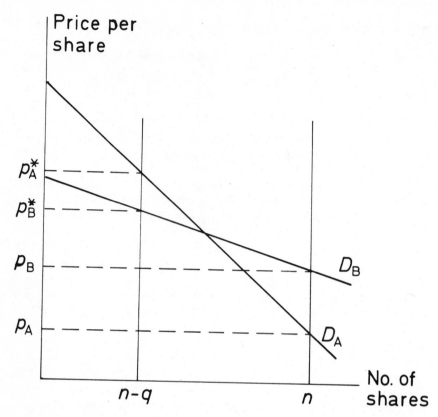

Figure 16-1. Market Demand Schedules for Two Policy Choices.

there exist two possible policy choices A and B. These are thought of as requiring the same amount of investment capital, so that the number of shares outstanding would be same under either alternative. Examples might be a choice between two different locations for starting oil drilling activities, or a shipping company's choice between short and long term charters for the same fleet. Suppose now that in Figure 16-1 the market demand schedules for the firm's shares look like the curves labelled D_A and D_B under policies A and B, respectively.[a] The given number of shares

[a] Some students are skeptical towards the possibility of there existing two policies with demand schedules such as those in Figure 16-1. However, this does not seem at all unreasonable. Suppose, for example, that individual demand functions are given by (12.2) and that firm j's output is uncorrelated with others. Then the market demand schedule is easily seen to be given by

$$p_j = \frac{1}{r}\left(\mu_j - R\sigma_{jj}\sum_i z_{ij}\right)$$

Two policies such that A has both larger mean and variance than B then typically give intersecting demand schedules.

outstanding is $\bar{n}$, and the policy that leads to the highest price per share is clearly policy B.

King assumes that a take-over bid has to be in the form of a public offer to buy shares at a stated price p_A^* or p_B^*, depending upon which policy is currently pursued. Suppose the number of shares needed to achieve a controlling interest in the firm is q; then plan A is the one requiring the highest offering price. Assuming that the firm's current management wishes to minimize the possibility of a successful take-over bid, we can conclude that policy A will be chosen, i.e., the policy giving the lowest share price in equilibrium.

For such an analysis to be meaningful it must clearly be assumed that none (or very few) of the existing shareholders are aware of (or believe in) the existence of another policy than the one currently being pursued. Apart from that, we have not taken into account the question of what the raider will do with his shares afterwards. If he can only sell them at the equilibrium price corresponding to the new policy, the conclusion above is reinforced: nobody in his right mind would buy shares at p_A^* and sell them at p_B. But this does not mean that the threat of a take-over would be any greater if the firm initially followed policy B: buying at p_B^*, changing to policy A and selling at p_A is not such a hot proposition either. Thus, regardless of which policy the firm pursues, it may be immune to a take-over bid.

Only if the raider can somehow practice perfect price discrimination, as suggested by Leland (by buying gradually up along one demand curve and selling down another) does it seem possible to make a profit on a take-over operation. But it is obvious that a profitable take-over operation is not necessarily one that involves changing the policy from one with a lower equilibrium price (policy A) to one with a higher (policy B); this will depend upon the location of the two demand curves relative to each other. If the current policy is A, and the demand curves intersect near $\bar{n} - q$, then a take-over and change to B may be profitable. If the current policy is B, and the demand curves intersect near $\bar{n}$, however, a takeover and change to A may very well be profitable.

The "analysis" above is neither complete nor elegant, and much remains to be done to get a satisfactory economic theory of take-overs.[b] But it does show that the traditional take-over argument is not as simple or straightforward as it may seem at first glance. It is not at all obvious that a raider can make a profit if the firm does not pursue a policy that maximizes the share price, and even a profitable take-over may result in a lower, rather than a higher, equilibrium price per share. Such observations may partly serve to explain the empirical fact that relatively few take-over bids (other than for purposes of effecting a merger) are successful.

---

[b] A game-theoretic approach, with the stockholders as players, seems promising in this regard.

16.3. As pointed out, phenomena such as take-overs presuppose the existence of disagreement among individuals with respect to an optimal policy for the firm. We shall use the rest of this chapter to consider stockholder disagreement more explicitly, particularly with a view to the role (if any) of share price maximization in achieving a solution. Unfortunately, little in the way of "hard" theoretical results seems to be available, and the treatment is therefore hardly more than exploratory.

16.4. We shall take as point of departure a very simplified model presented by King [1]. It is a model of an economy consisting of three individuals ($i = 1, 2, 3$) who face two investment opportunities: shareholdings in a risky firm and a riskless investment with zero interest. For the risky firm there is a choice between two production plans (A and B); these are again taken as requiring the same amount of investment, so that the number of shares is fixed. Riskless investment is also fixed at the level M. We assume three states of the world, and denote by

$X_k(\theta)$ — the firm's output in state θ ($\theta = 1, 2, 3$) under plan k ($k = A, B$).

p_k — the firm's market value under plan k.

$f_i(\theta)$ — individual i's probability distribution over states.

z_{ik} — porportion of the firm's shares held by individual i under plan k.

m_{ik} — individual i's riskless investment under plan k.

$Y_{ik}(\theta)$ — individual i's income in state θ under plan k.

An equilibrium allocation must clearly be such that

$$\sum_i z_{ik} = 1$$

and

$$\sum_i m_{ik} = M$$

The initial allocation is assumed to be the same for all individuals, so that the budget conditions are

$$m_{ik} + z_{ik}p_k = \frac{1}{3}(p_k + M)$$

With this, the $Y_{ik}(\theta)$ are given by

$$Y_{ik}(\theta) = z_{ik}X_k(\theta) + m_{ik}$$

$$= \frac{1}{3}(p_k + M) + z_{ik}[X_k(\theta) - p_k]$$

Furthermore, all individuals have the same utility function $u_i(Y_i) = \ln Y_i$; expected utilities are thus

$$U_{ik} = \sum_\theta \ln Y_{ik}(\theta) f_i(\theta)$$

The only difference among individuals is therefore different probability distributions $f_i(\theta)$.

16.5. We first derive the equilibrium allocation corresponding to any given production plan k. The first-order conditions for optimal portfolios under plan k are

$$\frac{\partial U_{ik}}{\partial z_{ik}} = \sum_\theta \frac{[X_i(\theta) - p_k] f_i(\theta)}{\frac{1}{3}(p_k + M) + z_{ik}[X_k(\theta) - p_k]} = 0$$

As a numerical example, we consider the output vectors shown in Table 16-1.

Under plan A, the optimality conditions take the form

$$\frac{p_A[1 - f_i(3)]}{\frac{1}{3}(p_A + M) - p_A z_{iA}} = \frac{(a - p_A) f_i(3)}{\frac{1}{3}(p_A + M) + (a - p_A) z_{iA}}$$

which can be solved for the optimal z_{iA} as

$$z_{iA} = \frac{(p_A + M)[a f_i(3) - p_A]}{3 p_A(a - p_A)}$$

Requiring

$$\sum_i z_{iA} = 1$$

we can then solve for the equilibrium company value as

$$p_A = \frac{aMF(3)}{a[1 - F(3)] + M}$$

where $F(\theta) \equiv \frac{1}{3}\Sigma_i f_i(\theta)$.

Under plan B the optimality conditions become

$$\frac{p_B[1 - f_i(1)]}{\frac{1}{3}(p_B + M) - p_B z_{iB}} = \frac{(b - p_B) f_i(1)}{\frac{1}{3}(p_B + M) + (b - p_B) z_{iB}}$$

Table 16-1
Numerical Example: Output Vectors for Two Investment Plans

	State		
	1	*2*	*3*
$X_A(\theta)$	0	0	a
$X_B(\theta)$	b	0	0

giving the optimal z_{iB} as

$$z_{iB} = \frac{(p_B + M)[bf_i(1) - p_B]}{3p_B(b - p_B)}$$

and the equilibrium value

$$p_B = \frac{bMF(1)}{b[1 - F(1)] + M}$$

To complete the numerical example, assume that $a = b = 10$, $M = 1$, and that the individuals' probability distributions are as shown in Table 16-2. This means that individuals 1 and 2 are identical, while individual 3 is the odd man out with a rather firm belief that state 3 will occur. This will clearly mean that he will have a strong preference in favor of plan A being adopted.

We can now, for each plan, compute the equilibrium value of the firm, the corresponding share allocation, and the resulting levels of expected utility. These are as shown in Table 16-3.

We observe, first of all, that plan A is the one that would give the highest equilibrium value of the firm, and we confirm that this plan would give individual 3 the highest level of expected utility. Individuals 1 and 2, however, have higher expected utilities under plan B: these individuals have a preference for income vectors with a lot in state 1, and the only way this can be obtained is by having the firm adopt plan B. Even though this plan gives them a budget of only ½—as compared to ⅔ under plan A—this is more than compensated for by the lower share price.

16.6. The next interesting observation is that both plans A and B are equilibrium solutions in the sense that they would receive majority stockholder support *ex post*, i.e., given the equilibrium shareholdings that are optimal relative to each plan. Thus suppose a particular plan is announced and trading takes place in the belief that this plan will be carried out. If shareholders are then allowed to vote on the choice of plan (without, however, having the possibility of trading again) then the chosen policy will receive majority support (plan A by 5/9 of the shares and plan B by 18/19).

Table 16-2
Individuals' Probability Distributions for the Numerical Example

	State		
	1	*2*	*3*
$f_1(\theta) = f_2(\theta)$	0.5	0.1	0.4
$f_3(\theta)$	0.1	0.05	0.85

Table 16-3
Resulting Allocations and Utilities for the Numerical Example

Allocations:

Plan	Value	Ind. 1 & 2	Ind. 3
A	$p_A = 1$	$z_{1A} = z_{2A} = 2/9$	$z_{3A} = 5/9$
B	$p_B = 1/2$	$z_{1B} = z_{2B} = 9/19$	$z_{3B} = 1/19$

Expected utilities:

Plan	Ind. 1 & 2	Ind. 3
A	−0.0942	1.1448
B	0.1372	−0.6725

But who is responsible for making the choice of plan in the first place and announcing it before trading takes place? We note that a majority of the original shareholders (i.e., given the initial allocation of one-third of the shares to each individual) would vote in favor of plan *B*. This support is based on the assumption of an irrevocable choice of plan with subsequent trading relative to that plan, in which case shareholders representing a two-thirds majority would come out better under plan *B* than plan *A*. King refers to this as *ex ante* stockholder support, and argues that on this basis plan *B* represents a stronger equilibrium concept.

Defining equilibrium concepts in terms of stockholder support as suggested above has some obvious shortcomings.

First of all, stockholder support is defined in terms of shareholdings that maximize expected utility given a particular choice of production plan for the firm, i.e., they represent a "passive" adaptation of individuals to a given production plan. This precludes from consideration the essentially dynamic nature of the process leading to a final choice of plan. We shall return to a discussion of this below.

Even granting the myopic nature of the given concepts of stockholder support, however, problems remain. Either directly (in the case of ex ante support) or indirectly (in the case of ex post support) the choice of plan depends crucially on the exogenously given initial allocation. The arbitrariness this introduces may or not be a serious objection, and it is by no means clear whether it is at all possible to define an equilibrium concept except relative to some given initial allocation.

A further problem with the concept of ex ante support is that the calculation of maximum expected utilities needed to determine the voting requires that individuals can predict (for each choice of production plan) the equilibrium prices at which the subsequent trading will take place.

Finally, our example suggests that majority voting to determine the production plan may not be very stable in that it could easily be short-circuited by side payments (or proxy-trading) among individuals. For example, we saw that with initial ownership of one-third each, individuals 1 and 2 could push through plan B and thus give themselves expected utility levels of 0.1372 each. Suppose now that individual 3 offers each an income vector $B(\theta)$ (for bribe) in return for relinquishing control of the firm to him so that he can put plan A in effect. To accept this, individuals 1 and 2 would require $B(\theta)$ to be such that

$$\sum_\theta \ln B(\theta) f_i(\theta) = 0.1372 \qquad (i = 1, 2)$$

Individual 3, on the other hand, would seek $B(\theta)$ such that

$$\sum_\theta \ln[X_A(\theta) + M - 2B(\theta)] f_3(\theta)$$

is a maximum. The solution to this constrained maximization problem is given by

$$B(\theta) = (0.4814, 0.4560, 4.2784)$$

This leaves individual 3 with the income vector

$$Y_3(\theta) = (0.0372, 0.0881, 2.4432)$$

with expected utility of $U_3 = 0.3087$. This, of course, is less than what he could have gotten if plan A had been determined in the first place, but a good deal better than if he had simply acquiesced to plan B.

16.7. We pointed out above the myopic nature of the solution concepts we have discussed so far. These concepts basically assume that individuals keep separate their decisions on optimal portfolio purchases (relative to a given production plan) and their decision on how to vote among production plans. Such separation obviously represents a poor description of the real world. If voting is to take place after the trading, then the individual's demand for shares will depend on his expectations with respect to the outcome of the voting. These expectations must in turn be based on estimates of other indivuduals' demand, which also depends on expectations about the outcome of the voting. The problems are to some extent similar to those encountered in traditional sequence economies where expectations about future prices affect demand in the spot market.

Share ownership serves two purposes: that of providing a claim to future income and that of defining voting power in the choice of production plan. This duality gives scope—perhaps more so than in ordinary commodity markets—for what we may call *strategic* stock purchases. By this we mean acquisitions motivated primarily by an interest in gaining control of the company and thereby actively influencing, or dictating, the choice of production plan. Let us return to our example and consider some possibilities.

Suppose we start with the initial allocationof one-third to each individual, and that plan B for some reason has been announced, but not irrevocably effected. Suppose further that individuals 1 and 2 are the suckers who believe that plan B will be effected, whereas individual 3 decides to acquire a majority interest in order to change the plan to A. If individual 3 decides to buy (say) a 53% interest, the equilibrium price must be such that $z_{1B} = z_{2B} = 0.235$; this determines $p_B = 1.439$. With this price and the given initial allocation, riskless investment will be 0.475 for individuals 1 and 2, and 0.050 for individual 3. After this trading has taken place, a new stockholders' meeting is called, and plan A is adopted. Consider now the following possibilities.

Possibility 1: Plan A is irrevocably effected, and all three individuals trade again with no strategic motives. The allocation given in the preceding paragraph is then taken as the initial allocation for the new trading. The new equilibrium price can then be calculated as $p_A = 0.9158$. At this price individual 3's optimal portfolio includes 48.84% of the firm's shares, i.e., a minority interest, and the corresponding level of expected utility is 0.9994. This is much better than if he were to adapt passively to plan B, but, because of the high price he had to pay in order to gain control of the firm, less than the situation where plan A had been adopted in the first place. Expected utilities for individuals 1 and 2 turn out to be -0.0302; this is slightly better than a situation where plan A had been adopted in the first place, but a good deal less than if plan B had been adhered to.

Possibility 2: Plan A is only tentatively decided upon, and individual 3 may decide to stick to his majority holding in order to prevent the others from changing the policy back to B. In that case his portfolio remains unchanged, and the resulting level of expected utility is 0.9772.

16.8. Examples such as these are hardly more than suggestive. One thing that *is* suggested is that the role of share price maximization in defining an equilibrium choice of production plan is far from obvious. What is more, stockholder disagreement is not necessarily a condition for conflict between share price maximization and stockholder interest. Ekern and Wilson demonstrated this for the evaluation of a marginal change in output satisfying the spanning property. King demonstrates that the possibility of unanimous rejection of the value maximizing choice of production plan also exists in the present model. This is done by considering the special case where all individuals are identical. We have already assumed identical initial allocations; we now also specify identical probability distributions, i.e., homogeneous expectations.

With $f_i(\theta) = f(\theta)$ for all i, we have $F(\theta) = f(\theta)$, and the equilibrium prices under the two plans become

$$p_A = \frac{aMf(3)}{a[1 - f(3)] + M}$$

$$p_B = \frac{bMf(1)}{b[1 - f(1)] + M}$$

From this we can deduce that p_A is higher than p_B if

$$\frac{f(1)}{f(3)} \leq \frac{a(M + b)}{b(M + a)}$$

Consider now expected utilities under the two plans. Since equilibrium portfolios are identical (i.e., $z_{iA} = z_{iB} = 1/3$ for all i) we have

$$Y_{ik}(\theta) = \frac{1}{3}[M + X_k(\theta)]$$

so that

$$U_{ik} = \sum_{\theta} \ln\left[\frac{1}{3}(M + X_k(\theta))\right] f(\theta)$$

Hence,

$$U_{iA} = [1 - f(3)] \ln \frac{M}{3} + f(3) \ln \frac{M + a}{3}$$

$$= \ln \frac{M}{3} + f(3) \ln \frac{M + a}{M}$$

and similarly

$$U_{iB} = \ln \frac{M}{3} + f(1) \ln \frac{M + b}{M}$$

for all i. From this we conclude that all individuals will prefer plan B to plan A if

$$\frac{f(1)}{f(3)} \geq \frac{\ln(M + a/M)}{\ln(M + b/M)}$$

Therefore, plan B has the lower equilibrium price, but is nevertheless unanimously supported by the stockholders if

$$\frac{\ln(M + a/M)}{\ln(M + b/M)} \geq \frac{f(1)}{f(3)} \geq \frac{a(M + b)}{b(M + a)}$$

A value for $f(1)/f(3)$ satisfying these inequalities exists whenever $b \geq a$.

Suppose, for example, that $M = 1$, $a = 10$, $b = 15$; the inequalities are then

$$0.8649 \leq \frac{f(1)}{f(3)} \leq 0.9697 .$$

A probability distribution satisfying this would be

$$f(\theta) = (0.36, 0.24, 04.0)$$

We would then have

$$p_A = 0.5714, \qquad p_B = 0.5094$$

but

$$U_{iA} = -0.1395, \qquad U_{iB} = -0.1005$$

for every i.

16.9. From the vantage point of this simple model we shall conclude our analysis of the optimality of investment by exploring once more the source of conflict between share price maximization on the one hand and stockholder interests and Pareto-optimality on the other. In earlier sections we have attributed this discrepancy to the existence of exclusive investment rights for the firm. That this may lead to an allocation that is not Pareto-optimal is a readily acceptable proposition which has its obvious counterpart in traditional market theory. But why is it that share price maximization may be contrary to the owners' interests? Clearly, the higher the share price, the higher the stockholder's initial wealth and the larger his budget. Why, then would the owners of a firm not wish to have the value of their wealth maximized? And why is it that such a proposition does not seem to have a counterpart in traditional commodity markets under uncertainty? We are quite familiar with the idea that profit maximization for a monopoly may lead to a welfare loss on the part of consumers, but few have questioned the *owner's* interest in profit maximization.

Clearly, if a stockholder does not wish to have his wealth maximized, there must be some kind of externality or indirect benefit from having the firm pursue a different policy. Such a benefit arises because the firm's choice of production plan affects the prices of the goods that he is implicitly purchasing. We have repeatedly pointed out that with incomplete markets, claims to income in different states of the world cannot be bought directly but only as composite goods in the form of stocks and bonds. Corresponding to any optimal income vector, there exists, for each individual, a set of implicit prices for state contingent claims, namely, the prices that would have made the individual buy the portfolio $Y_i(\theta)$ of state contingent claims if such claims had in fact been available. It is when the firm's choice of production plan affects these prices that indirect benefits from a production plan that does not maximize his wealth may occur.

To find the implicit prices for state contingent claims in our example, we can proceed as follows. With a complete set of state contingent claims, the individual's optimization problem is to find $Y_i(\theta)$ so as to maximize Σ_θ ln $Y_i(\theta)f_i(\theta)$ subject to the budget condition

$$\sum_\theta \pi(\theta)Y_i(\theta) = W_i$$

It is easily verified that the solution to this problem is given by

$$Y_i(\theta) = W_i \frac{f_i(\theta)}{\pi(\theta)}$$

For each individual with a given income vector and budget (under a given production plan), the implicit prices of state congingent claims can therefore be calculated as

$$\pi_i(\theta) = W_i \frac{f_i(\theta)}{Y_i(\theta)}$$

The resulting prices for the numerical example are given in Table 16-4. For example, under plan A, $W_i = 2/3$ for all individuals, and for individuals 1 and 2 we have $Y_i(\theta) = (4/9, 4/9, 1/9)$; hence the price vector becomes $\pi_i(\theta) = (0.75, 0.15, 0.10)$, etc.

The impact of the choice of production plan on relative prices for income in different states of the world is in this example quite clear. Under plan A, which gives a large output in state 3, the prices for income in state 3 are low; under plan B the opposite is true.

The significance of this is that when choosing a production plan the stockholder must keep in mind not only the impact on the value of his wealth but also on the prices of the goods he wishes to purchase. The traditional argument for the proposition that share price maximization is in every stockholder's interest (because it brings him on the highest possible

Table 16-4
Implicit Prices for State Contingent Claims

	Ind. 1 & 2			Ind. 3		
	State			State		
	1	2	3	1	2	3
Plan A	0.75	0.15	0.10	0.60	0.30	0.10
Plan B	0.05	0.19	0.76	0.05	0.0528	0.8972

budget line) is most certainly based on the assumption that relative prices are given (i.e., that the budget lines corresponding to different wealth levels are parallel). When the policy choice also affects the slope of the budget lines, unambiguous welfare implications are not to be expected.

The quantitative importance of the effect on implicit prices obviously depends on the "size" of the firm in relation to the economy as a whole. Thus, in our example, it is easy to show that if we let M become large relative to a and b, the difference in prices under different plans becomes less pronounced, since then the impact of the firm's decision is smaller.

16.10. It is clear that these results derive not from uncertainty in itself but rather from the monopoly position of the firm as supplier of goods that the individual purchases. A proposition of the same kind should therefore hold with respect to monopolies in ordinary commodity markets under uncertainty.

Suppose you are a stockholder in a monopoly producing ale and beer. Suppose further that this firm has a choice between two production plans: plan A, which would include a large output of ale and very little beer, and plan B with very little ale and a lot of beer. With plan A the equilibrium price of ale would be very low and that of beer very high; with plan B there would be the opposite pattern. Suppose finally that plan A is the one yielding the higher profit. Then it is clear that the size of your budget is larger if plan A is adopted. However, if you love beer and detest ale it may perfectly well be to your advantage to have the firm adopt plan B. And if you have enough brothers in spirit, you may be able to vote out a management proposing to do otherwise.

We noted that such effects generally seem to have been overlooked. This is because we tend to treat the "firm" as a separate entity and ignore the composition of its owners and their role as consumers. These interrelationships may not be quantitatively important in a highly developed competitive economy, but appears to have been quite significant in the earlier stages of industrial development. The nature of the problem was in fact alluded to by Marshall [3, p. 486]

... a railway company ... finds its own interests so closely connected with those of the purchasers of its services, that it gains by making some temporary sacrifice of net revenue with the purpose of increasing consumers' surplus.

References

1. King, M., "Equilibrium Concepts in Stock Market Economies," paper presented to the Third World Congress of the Econometric Society, Toronto, August 1975.

2. Leland, H.E., "Production Theory and the Stock Market," *Bell Journal of Economics and Management Science*, 1974, pp. 125-144.

3. Marshall, A., *Principles of Economics*, 8th Ed. London: Macmillan & Co., 1920.

Index

arbitrage profit, 37, 81, 88
Arrow-Debreu securities. *See* state
    contingent claims
asset proportions, 65, 73

bankruptcy. *See* default
Borch, K.H., 9, 13

capital structure, 83-94, 99-102
Cass, D., 66, 71
complete markets: definition of, 37; de-
    cision making in, 32-37; model
    of, 22-24, 29; Pareto optimality
    in, 25-27, 32

default, 83, 92
demand schedule for shares, 105, 123,
    144
Diamond, P., 103-110, 110, 117, 122,
    124, 130, 141
distributive efficiency, 43, 97
dividend, 21

Ekern, S., 124, 127, 132, 133
entry, free, 140
equilibrium, attainment of, 17, 36

feasibility constraints, 6, 23, 30
financial equilibrium, 127, 133
firms, 5, 155
Fisher's rule of intertemporal alloca-
    tion, 12

Hakansson, N.H., 78, 81
homogeneous expectations, 49, 61, 73,
    78, 113

Jensen, M.C., 110, 117, 125, 133-138,
    141

King, M.A., 143, 145, 146-153, 156
Kuhn-Tucker theorem, 9

Leland, H.E., 127, 132, 145, 156

Lintner, J., 109
Long, J., 110, 117, 125, 133-138, 141

market imperfections, 83, 138
market index, 117
market manager, 17
market portfolio. *See* perfectly bal-
    anced portfolio
market risk aversion factor, 114, 118,
    122, 124
Marshall, A., 156
mean-variance efficient portfolios, 78,
    109, 111-112
merger, 86
Merton, R.C., 110, 133, 138-141, 142
Miller, M.H., 83, 94
Modigliani, F., 83, 94
Modigliani-Miller propositions, 83, 87-
    91, 97
monopolistic elements, 123, 138, 155-
    156
Mossin, J., 78, 81, 109

opportunity set, change in, 87, 91

Pareto-optimality, 7-13; attainability
    of, 53, 54-64; constrained, 47, 48-
    49, 109; departure from, 122, 132,
    137
perfect competition, 138, 140
perfectly balanced portfolios, 59, 73,
    86, 115, 133
production function, stochastic, 5; de-
    composable, 36, 104, 109, 124;
    spanning property of, 128-129;
    Stiglitz's 117, 131
proportionality assumption, 104, 109,
    122, 141
proxy: fight, 143; trading, 150
public offering of shares, 100

returns to scale, 5, 24, 106, 133, 141
rights issue, 100
risk class, 83

157

riskfree investment, 5, 24
risk measure for firm, 114, 118, 122, 139
risk tolerance function, 61, 66, 73, 78, 115

secondary markets, 45
separation property, 53, 65-71
shadow market, 32, 79
share price maximization, 99, 143, 148, 151, 153
Sharpe, W.F., 109, 117, 125
single-commodity assumption, 3
SLM-model, 109, 111-115
state contingent claims, 18, 79; implicit prices for, 154; imputed prices for, 32, 37, 79
state of the world, 5; number of, 37-40, 79-81; probability distributions over, 11

Stiglitz, J.E., 66, 71, 84, 94, 110, 117-124, 125, 131, 133, 138
stochastic dependence, 5, 109, 117
stockholder support, 149. *See also* unanimity proposition
strategic stock acquisitions, 151
Subrahmanyam, M.G., 110, 133, 138-141, 142

take-over bids, 143-146
two-period assumption, 3

unanimity proposition, 127-132
utility function, 11; logarithmic, 78; quadratic, 78, 115

Wilson, R., 124, 127, 132, 133

About the Author

Jan Mossin is Professor of Business Administration at the Norwegian School of Economics and Business Administration, Bergen, Norway. He received the Ph.D. from Carnegie-Mellon University, and has had visiting appointments at University of California, Berkeley, New York University, and Columbia University. His publications include *Theory of Financial Markets* and a number of articles in the area of financial economics. Professor Mossin is a fellow of the Econometric Society, and a board member of the European Finance Association.